St. Helens Pals

11th (Service) Battalion South Lancashire Regiment
(St. Helens Pioneers)

War Diary

Edited by David Risley

Lancashire Infantry Museum

First published in the United Kingdom in 2016 by

Lancashire Infantry Museum

ISBN:9781541244610

St. Helens Pals

War Diary

Contents

Acknowledgements

The editor gratefully acknowledges the assistance of the following in gathering research material, granting permission to use copyright material, and providing invaluable assistance in various ways:

The Lancashire Infantry Museum for granting access to their archives. In particular Jane Davies, Archivist, and Major (retd) Douglas Farrington for his help with South Lancashire Regiment archives.

I would also like to thank Charles Fair for his help with Divisional and R.E. records held at Kew.

David Risley

1 August 2016

Introduction

This is the fourth in a series of volumes arising from a project to research 11th Battalion South Lancashire Regiment, the St. Helens Pals. Its aim is to make available the battalion's War Diary, supplemented with other relevant, official material.

Where material has been added from other sources, e.g. Commonwealth War Graves Commission, Divisional War Diaries, R.E. War Diaries, etc., the source is referenced in square brackets [...].

Where the text is shaded and/or consists of dots, e.g. '.....', this indicates material that is difficult to read or, in fact, unreadable or missing due to damage to the original document.

As this volume is in portrait and the original often in landscape, some 'ditto's in the original have been replaced by the wording from the line above to aid clarity.

Maps

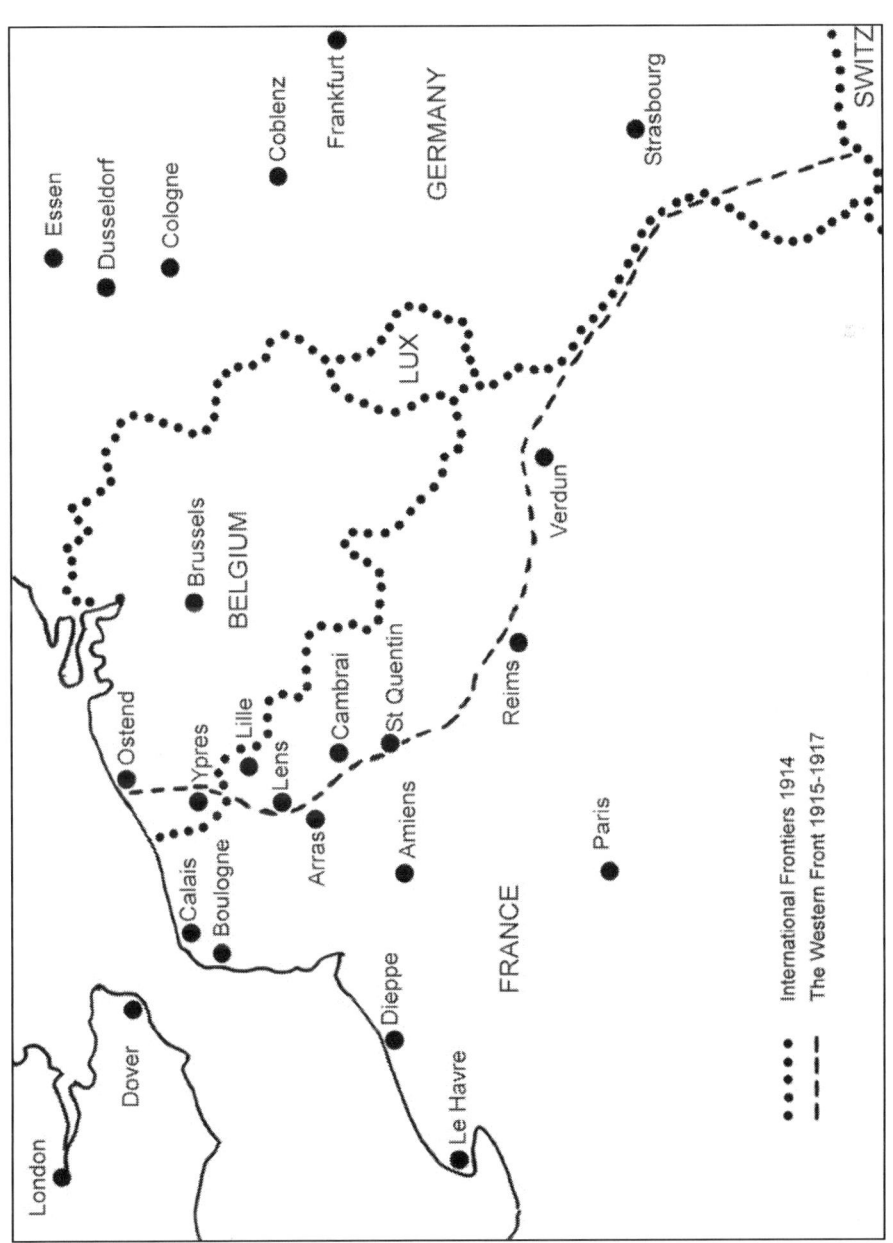

The Western Front, 1915-1917

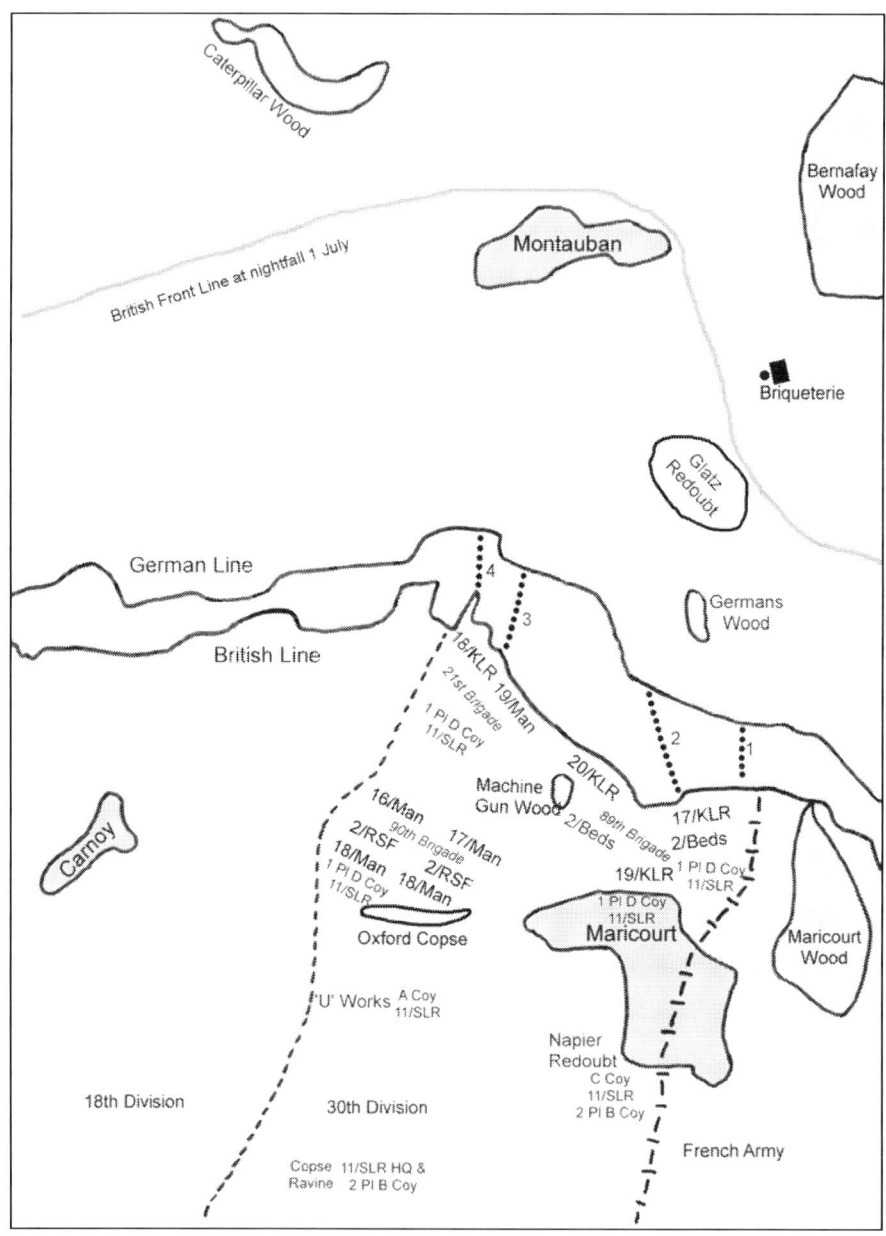

30th Division position, 30 June 1916
Infantry positions and the four saps dug by 11th South Lancs on 1 July

The Somme Offensive, 1 July - 6 November 1916

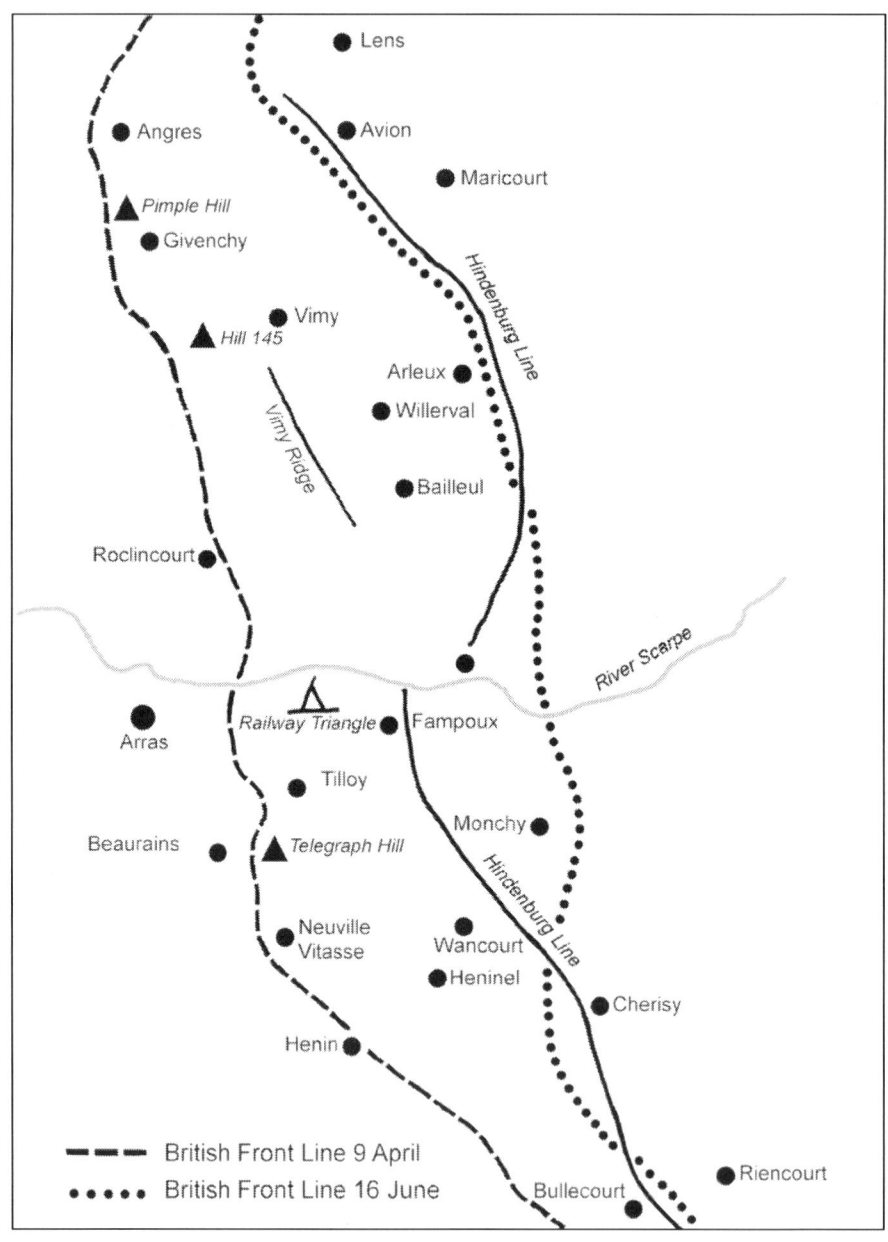

The Arras Offensive, 9 April - 16 June 1917

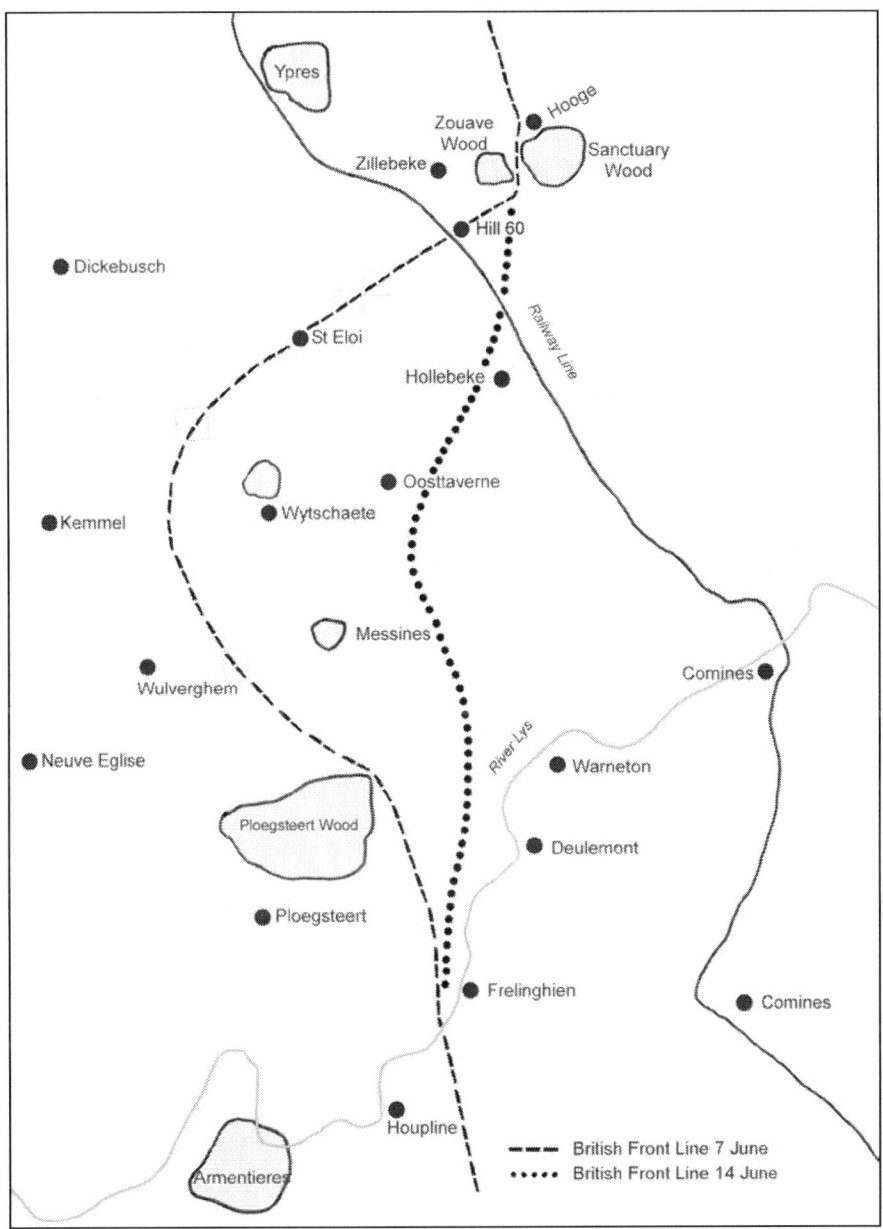

The Battle of Messines, 7 - 14 June 1917

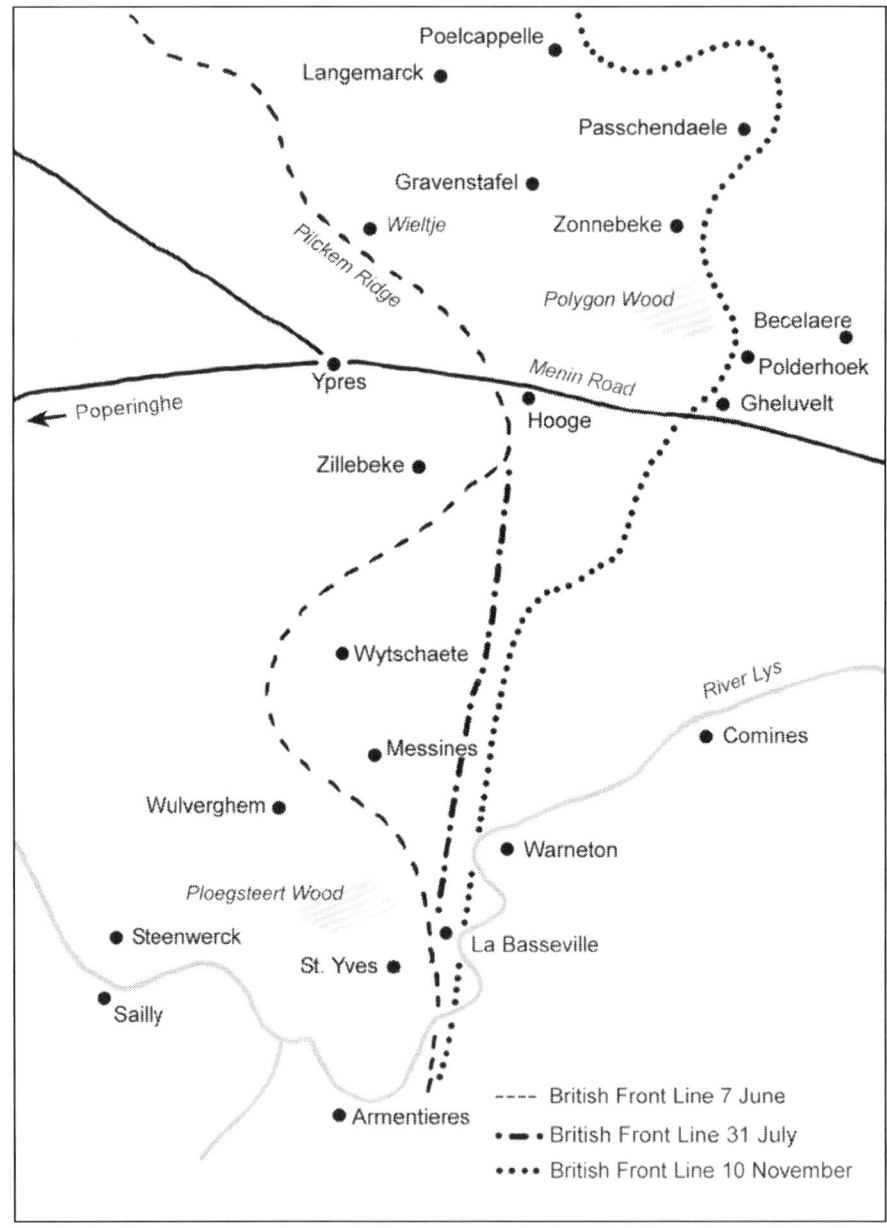

The Third Battle of Ypres (Passchendaele), 31 July - 10 November 1917

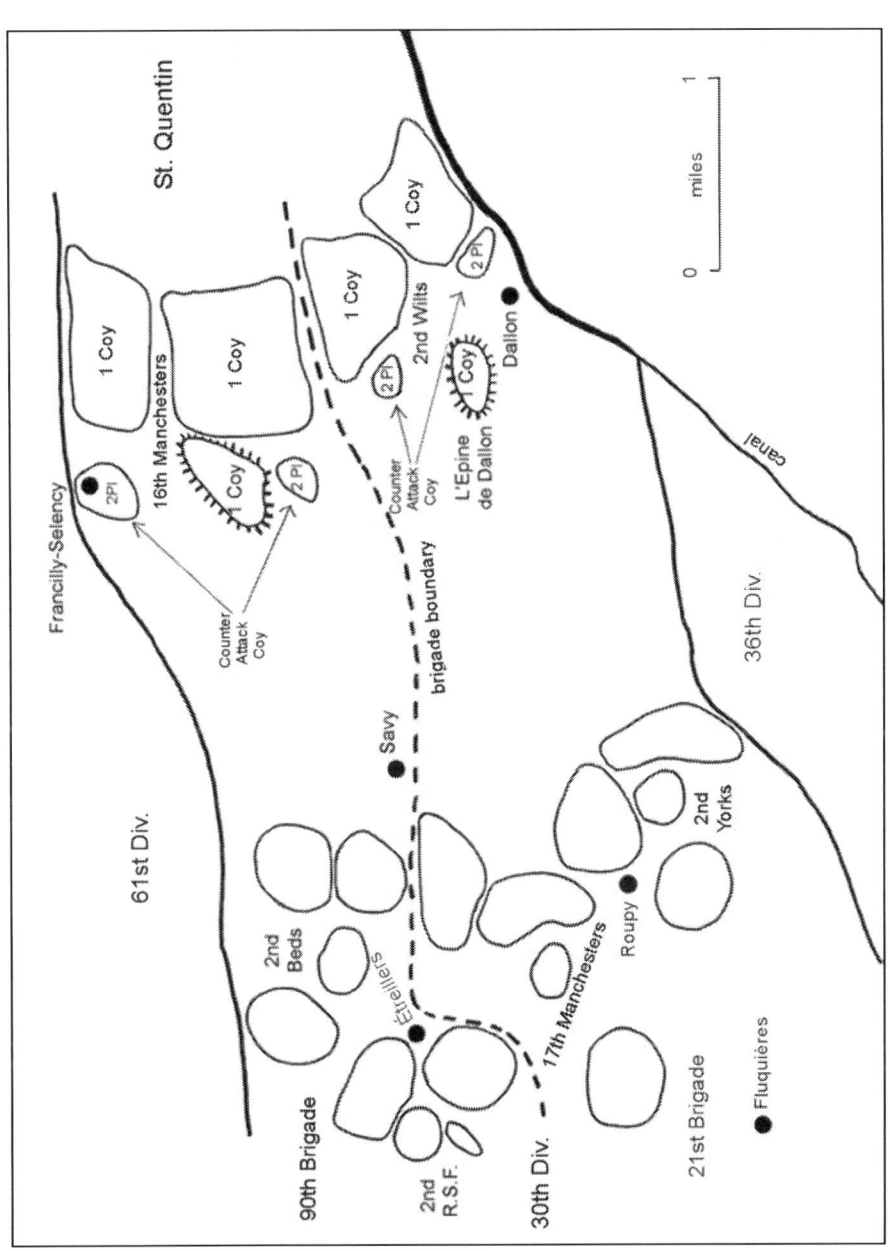

St. Quentin

1 Coy

16th Manchesters

1 Coy

1 Coy

1 Coy

2 Pl

2nd Wilts

Counter
Attack
Coy

L'Epine
de Dallon

1 Coy

Dallon

2 Pl

2 Pl

1 Coy

Francilly-Selency

Counter
Attack
Coy

canal

brigade boundary

36th Div.

Savy

61st Div.

2nd
Yorks

2nd
Beds

Étreillers

Roupy

17th Manchesters

21st Brigade

90th Brigade

2nd
R.S.F.

30th Div.

Fluquières

30th Division positions, 21 March 1918

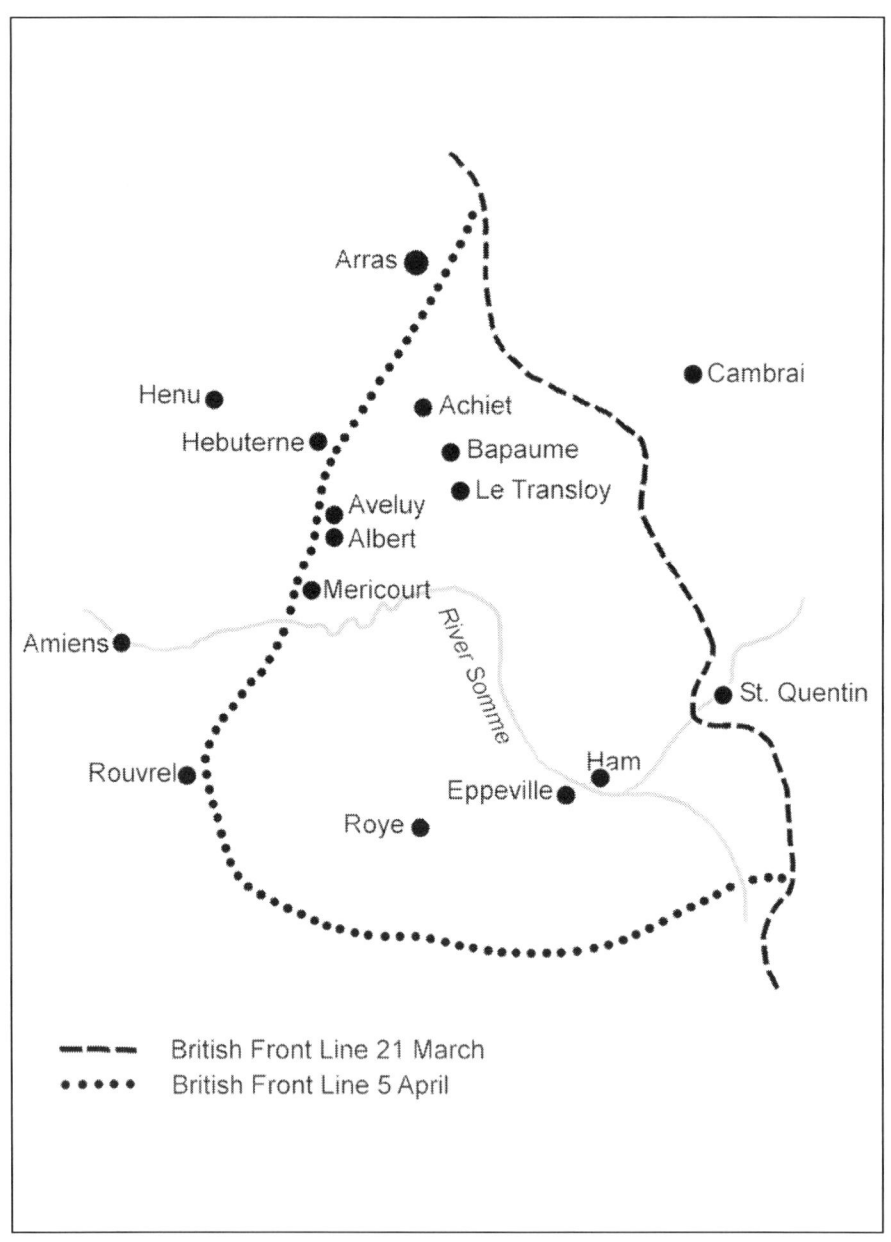

Operation Michael, March 1918

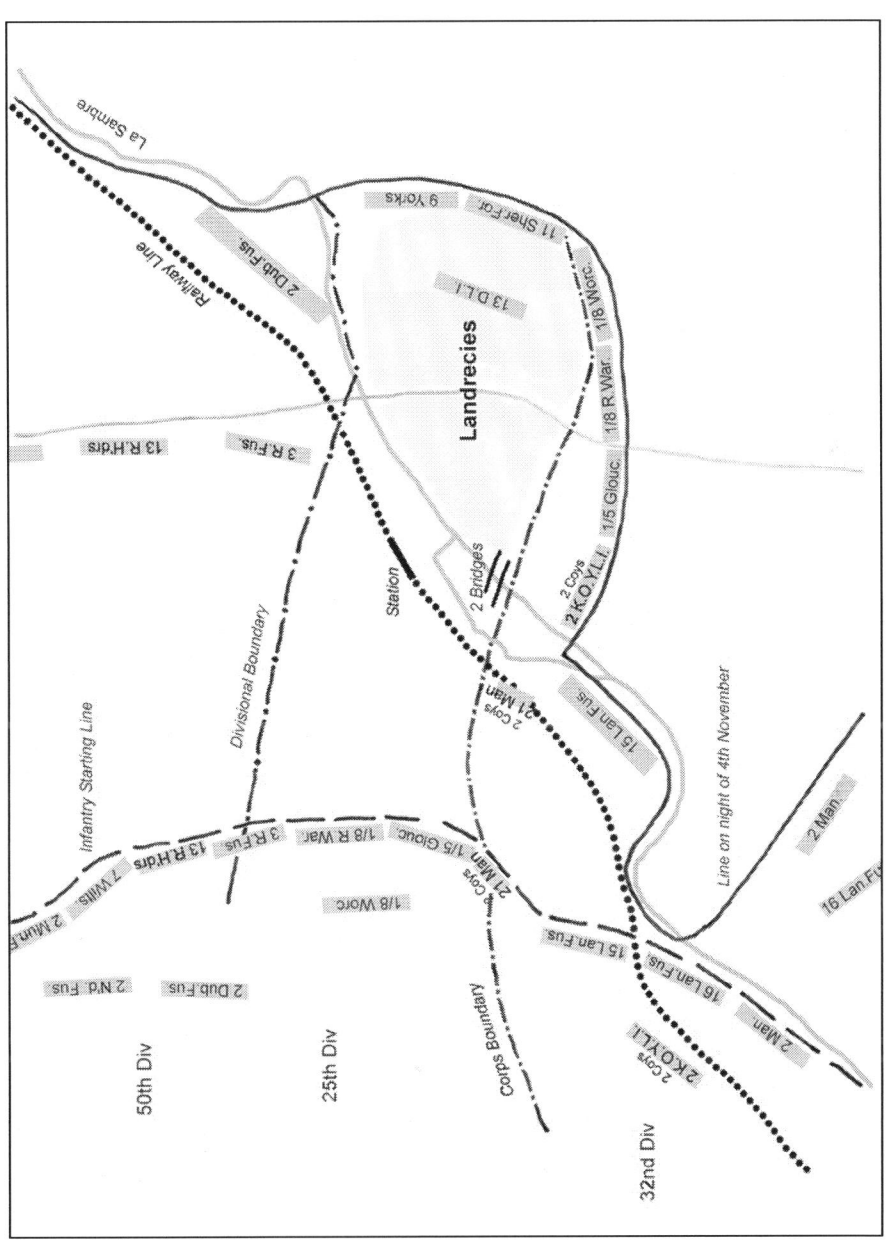

The Battle of the Sambre-Oise Canal, 4 November 1918

1915

Place	Date	Hour	Summary of Events and Information
Larkhill Camp	06/11		Left Larkhill Camp on 6th Nov for Southampton
Southampton	06/11	15:00	Embarked on "MONAS QUEEN" & sailed at 5pm. Transport on "Invicta".
Le Havre	07/11	00:00	Arrived at Havre at 12 midnight & disembarked at 8.0am on the 7.11.15.
		08:00	Proceeded to Rest Camp about 2 miles outside HAVRE.
		19:30	Left Rest Camp, Havre at 7.30 p.m. and proceeded to place of Entrainment "GARE des MERCHANDISES"
		23:59	Left at 11.59pm and arrived at PONT REMY at 6.30am on the 8.11.15.
Pont Remy	08/11	06:30	Strength arrived at PONT REMY 29 Officers 1007 O. Ranks. 1 Officer & 1 O. Ranks left behind HAVRE as Divisional Embark'n Officer.
		07:30	Marched out of PONT REMY for Busses Bussuel at 7.30am 8/11/15 about 8 miles from Station. (Note) In Full Marching Order plus Blanket & W.P. Sheet.
Bussus Bussuel	08/11	16:00	Arr Bussus Bussuel about 4pm 8/11/15. Rest on way & a meal given to men. Road bad.
Bethencourt	16/11		Left Bussus Bussuel on the 16th Nov for BETHENCOURT arriving & billeted by 3pm.
			Departed on 17th Nov & arr FLESSELLES at 1pm same day.
Flesselles	17/11		On way from Bethencourt to Flesselles we met the 5th S. Lancs & formed up in line & as 5th S Lancs approached us we gave 3 Rousing Cheers for them to which they heartily reciprocated. Fell out for 1/2 hr for chat.
Flesselles	26/11		2 Coys ('A' & 'B') left for MAILLY MAILLET

1

Place	Date	Hour	Summary of Events and Information
Mailly Maillet			on 26/11/15 at 9.0am for instruction in Trenches and attached to 10th Bde 4th Divn.
			Stgth 11 Officers 444 O Ranks.
			Returned from Trenches on 11th Decr. No casualties.
Flesselles Berneuil	28/11	09:10 12:30	'C', 'D' Coys & Hd Qrs left Flesselles at 9.10am & arrived at BERNEUIL at 12.30 same day.
	06/12		'C' Coy left BERNEUIL for HALLOY-LES-PERNOIS for work on Horse standings in Artillery Area. 6 Offrs & 223 O.R.
	10/12		'C', 'D' & Hd Qrs left on 10th Decr for training in Trenches attchd 10th Bde - 4th Divn. 'C' Coy joined 'D' & Hd Qrs at Le Val de Maison at 12.45 on 10th Decr.
	12/12		'D' Coy (7 Off & 134 OR) went in Trenches for 3 days and 3 nights.
			'C' Coy (6 Off & 165 OR) working parties.
	13/12		'C' Coy (6 Off & 165 OR) working parties & were sniped freely by enemy.
			Enemy aircraft over MAILLY MAILLET and dropped 2 Bombs in village 1 failed to go off, other exploded near Coy Billets but did no damage.
	14/12		'C' Coy (6 Off & 165 OR) working parties. 2 men wounded through enemy sniping.
	16/12		[d.o.w. Pte. 20523 Joseph Beard]
	19/12		'C' Coy go in trenches for 3 days and 3 nights & portion of 'D' Coy. 'D' Coy working parties for Trenches. 2 men wounded by enemy snipers. 1 man killed by enemy sniper.
			[k.i.a. Pte. 21005 Harry Taylor]
	20/12		'D' Coy 1 man killed by enemy sniper & 1 wounded - died 21/12/15.

Place	Date	Hour	Summary of Events and Information
			[k.i.a. Pte. 21325 Frederick Cartwright]
	21/12		1 man died of Alcoholic Poisoning at BERNEUIL when on Guard. (Pte. P Critchley) L/Corpl i/c Guard remanded for F.G.C.M.
			[d. Pte. 21793 Peter Critchley; d.o.w. Pte. 20949 Louis Lambert, Pte. 21481 John Stanley]
	24/12		[k.i.a. Pte. 20995 William Groves]
	25/12	09:00	Left MAILLY MAILLET on 25th Decr for BERNEUIL via PUCHEVILLERS.
	27/12	09:30	Left BERNEUIL as follows Hd Qrs & 'B' Coy to PERNOIS 'A' Coy Artillery Area
			'C' Coy to OUTREBOIS.
			'D' Coy HEM & HARDINVAL
			Split up in this manner for various work on improvements to Billets &c.
	31/12	11:30	L/C Smith to be tried by F.G.C.M. in BERNAVILLE.

1916

Place	Date	Hour	Summary of Events and Information
	01/01		Battalion divided as per end of last Summary.
Pernois	05/01		Left Pernois at 9.45am & marched to NAOURS ('A' & 'B' Coys & Hd Qrs) 'C' & 'D' Coys meeting us there.
Pont Noyelles	06/01		Battn left NAOURS at 8.50am & marched to PONT NOYELLES
	07/01		Battn left PONT NOYELLES at 8.30am (less 'A' Coy) & marched to CHIPILLY ('C' & 'D') & ETINEHAM ('B' & Hd Qrs).
			'A' Coy left PONT NOYELLES for PUCHEVILLERS for Railway work under R.C.E. 112th Railway Coy RE
	08/01		Battn less 'A' Coy marched to BRAY 'D' Coy proceeding to SUZANNE 'B' 'C' & H Qrs to FROISSY
	11/01		'D' Coy at SUZANNE had 2 casualties (wounded in action) Enemy shelling Artillery there. 'B' 'C' Coys working on BRAY-CORBIE Road, BRONFAY Fme Light Railway
	14/01		Machine Gun Section proceeded to SUZANNE for work under G.O.C. 90th Brigade.
	16/01		Work commenced on light railway BRONFAY FARM - Point 104 by 11th. South Lancs (Pioneer) Battalion. 2 Platoons 11th. South Lancs commenced road repairs on main BRAY-CORBIE road. 2½ Platoons commenced repairs and clearing in CARNOY AVENUE. [30th Division C.R.E. War Diary]

NOMINAL ROLL OF OFFICERS

11th (S) Bn. South Lancashire Regt. (Pioneers).

Lieut. Colonel:	Harrington, Sir J.L., K.C.M.G., K.C.V.O., C.B.
Major:	Gwyn-Williams, R.H. Potter, T.
Captain:	Champion, A.T. Burn, R.W. Bury, R.F. Dixon, C.J. Champion, C.C. Forester, T.
Lieutenant:	Fletcher, J.N. Walker, G.H. Garton, R.W. Woolcock, H.J. Woods, S.E.
2nd Lieutenant:	Diplock, A.B. Craig, F. Bretherton, W. Parsons, J. Walker, A.D. Culshaw, J.G. Williams, R. Champion, E.O. Fletcher, W.G. Miller, R.W.R. Dean, A.G. Bradley, A.
Adjutant:	Captain Brooke, H.K.
Quartermaster:	Lieutenant Rice, A.H.N.
Medical Officer:	Lieutenant Kuny, S.
Machine Gun Officer:	Lieutenant Buchanan, R.B.

[30th Division A&Q War Diary]

Place	Date	Hour	Summary of Events and Information
Froissy	21/01	18:50	Shelled by Enemy on 21/1/16 at irregular intervals 1 man wounded.
	22/01		2 Platoons of 11th Bn. South Lancs Regt. Commenced work in improving and clearing SHEFFIELD AVENUE. [30th Division C.R.E. War Diary]
Froissy	24/01	16:00	5 shells sent over. 2 Mules wounded.
Froissy	25/01	15:20	11 shells sent over. No casualties.
Froissy	26/01	15:50	8 Shells over Froissy.
		16:20	5 " " "
Froissy	27/01	10:58 11:00	8 shells. 0 casualties. End of Hut just behind Bn Hd Qrs blown in.
		14:23	4 shells (1 did not go off). Mark on Fuse Cap HZ 14 & 15 apparently fired by 10.5 Light Field Howitzer from direction of FAY.
Suzanne	28/01		1 man wounded of 'D' Coy. This Coy under orders of G.O.C. 90th Bde.
Froissy	28/01	07:18 16:00	Continually shelled by Enemy, but the majority of shells were somewhat over-ranged falling in a field behind the Bn Hd Qrs. 685 shells were sent over at an average of 1 per minute. 1 man killed 1 wounded.
			Ordered by Division (30th) to move out of FROISSY this being done about 4.30p.m. About 2pm Artillery was exceedingly active, the enemy attempting to break through the Left of the Trench Lines & Right of our Lines.
			[k.i.a. Pte. 21144 John Mason]
	29/01		Communication trench to provide covered communication between SUZANNE and BRAY was started by a detachment of 11th B. South Lancs Regt. [30th Division C.R.E. War Diary]
Bray	30/01		Working Parties detailed for urgent work at CAPPY placing Houses in state of Defence,

Place	Date	Hour	Summary of Events and Information
			making Machine Gun Emplacements & Redoubts.
	31/01		Ditto -------------- Ditto --------------------
Bray	03/02		On 3/2/16 'A' Coy arrived at ETINEHEM from PUCHEVILLERS and joined Battalion for duty. Left Billets in BRAY (2 Coy & HQ) & moved to DUGOUTS. Position L8 Map 62C N.W. ALBERT.
	07/02		'A' Coy took over duties from 'D' Coy at SUZANNE. 'D' Coy moved to ETINEHEM.
	09/02		'D' Coy moved into DUGOUTS with Battalion Hd Qrs.
	14/02		[d.o.w. Pte. 20958 George Hood]
	18/02		1 man wounded 'A' Coy.
	20/02		[d.o.w. Pte. 20210 Thomas Myers]
	21/02		1 man wounded 'A' Coy & 1 of 'C' Coy.
	29/02		1 man wounded 'B' Coy & died shortly after & 1 man wounded 'A' Coy.
			During month work on Communication Trenches & making Dugouts SUZANNE & making Dugouts at Bn Hd Qrs to take whole of Battalion. Continuation of work at CAPPY placing same in State of Defence & work in Front Line Trenches.
Suzanne	01/03		1 Man 'A' Coy wounded at SUZANNE.
			[d.o.w. Pte. 20486 Robert Howard]
Bray	10/03		1 Man 'D' Coy wounded.
			[d.o.w. Pte. 20145 John Mills]
Suzanne	11/03		1 Man 'A' Coy wounded at SUZANNE slightly but returned 12/3/16.
	14/03		Major Gwynn Williams 2nd Comd invalided to England 13/3/16 & struck off strength.
	15/03		'A' Coy joined Battn at Dugouts Grovetown

Place	Date	Hour	Summary of Events and Information
			Camp Bray on 15th inst.
	16/03		'A' & 'D' Coys leave Dugouts & march to 7th Div Area at MEAULTE. Hd Qrs to VILLE sur ANCRE.
			"B & 'C' Coys move out of Dugouts to Tents on Bank opposite to allow the Sussex Regt Pioneers to occupy.
Meaulte	19/03		1 NCO & 2 men 'A' Coy wounded by Shell Fire. NCO suffered from Shell Shock he has however returned to duty.

STATEMENT OF CASUALTIES
PERIOD 8th JANUARY to 20th MARCH (inclusive)

11th South Lancs. Regt. Killed: 2 O.R. Wounded 12 O.R. Total 14 O.R.
[30th Division A&Q War Diary]

Place	Date	Hour	Summary of Events and Information
Meaulte	27/03		2 men wounded 'A' Coy owing to Shellfire. 1 since returned to duty.
	31/03		'A' & 'D' Coys & Hd.Qrs. left Meaulte & Ville respectively & went back to GROVETOWN (under Canvas).
			Comg Officer sick & has to leave Battn for rest. Major T Potter taking over Command from that date.
	03/04		Dug new Fire Trench in front of front line at Pt F 11 27 & F 11 3 from 1.30 pm to 5 am. 298 NCO & men of 'B' & 'C' Coys & 7 Officers took part. Trench completed & manned by 21st Manchester Regt.
			Working parties carried on day & night.
	18/04		Move back to VAUX en AMIENOIS for rest.
	27/04		Inspection by Divisional Comr Major Genl W Fry CNQCB at 9.30 am. On parade 25 Officers 856 Other Ranks.

Place	Date	Hour	Summary of Events and Information
Vaux en Amienois	02/05	08:50	'B' & 'C' Coys under Capt Forester left for BOIS de Celestine nr Chipilly.
			'C' Coy & 1/2 'B' Coy on road work under Officer i/c Roads 13th Corps at Bois de Tailles; 1/2 'B' Coy under O.C. 142nd Coy.
	03/05	16:00	'A' & 'D' Coys & HQ left Vaux en Amienois at 4pm for Corbie & billetted there for the night.
Corbie	04/05	16:00	Left Corbie at 4.0pm for Grovetown Camp.
	06/05		'A' Coy (2 platoons) went to SUZANNE.
		16:30	'B' & 'C' Coys rejoined Battn at Grovetown Camp. 'C' Coy went on to SUZANNE.
	07/05		'B' Coy to "F" Ravine.
	11/05 13/05		77 NCO's & men 'C' Coy engaged on Rescue Work in Trench Y3 commencing 5.30pm on 11th continuing in hourly reliefs until 13/5/16.
	16/05		Lt Col Sir J L Harrington KCMG, KCVO, CB, comdg Battn went to England (Sick Leave). Whilst there received notification from XIII Corps that he had received appointment as Commandant ARDRICQUE.
	18/05		1 man 'A' Coy wounded (Shrapnel) returned to duty 25/5/16.
	19/05		1 man 'C' Coy wounded.
			1 Platoon 'D' Coy moved to "F" Ravine on 19th inst.
	23/05		1 man 'D' Coy wounded
			1 man 'B' Coy wounded slightly. Returned to duty 27/5/16.
	26/05		Lt Col H. F. Fenn (late 21st Royal Fusrs) reported & took over command of Battalion.
	30/05		2 Platoons 'A' Coy & remainder 'D' Coy moved to TRIGGER VALLEY.
	31/05		Distribution of Battn evening of 31/5/16:-

Place	Date	Hour	Summary of Events and Information
			11 Platoons in Trigger Valley 5 Platoons in "F" Ravine. Bn Hd Qrs in GROVETOWN DUGOUTS.
			2 men wounded 1 of C & 1 of D.
Etinehem	01/05 31/05		During this period a considerable amount of work was carried out by Field Companies and the Pioneer Battalion under the C.R.E.'s direction. It consisted almost entirely of preparing the Division front for active operations by the construction of trenches, shelters, assembly places, battle headquarters, etc. [30th Division C.R.E. War Diary]
	01/06		Dist'n of Battn
			TRIGGER VALLEY 11 Platoons ('A' & 'C' Coy & pns 'D' Coy)
			F RAVINE 4 Platoons ('B' Coy)
			DIV Dugouts 1 Platoons ('D' Coy) N E of Bray.
			Bn HQ TRIGGER VALLEY
			QM Stores & Transport BRAY
	03/06		1 NCO ('D' Coy) wounded.
	04/06		21435 Sgt P. McGowan 'C' Coy tried by F. G. Court Martial for "When on Active Service Drunkenness" Sentence Reduced to the Ranks.
			Lt & QM Rice struck off strength effect from 2/6/16 2Lt F Craig transferred to 3 Hussars 6/6/16.
			[d.o.w. Pte. 20569 Thomas Roberts]
	06/06		Capt C. C. Champion appd Temy Major & 2nd in Command of Battn effect from 14/4/16.
	08/06		2 men wounded 'B' Coy.
	11/06		2Lt A. G. R. Hawkes invalided to England.

Place	Date	Hour	Summary of Events and Information
			20086 Pte Pounceby W 'B' Coy awarded Military Medal vide London Gazette 3/6/16. (1st decoration for Battn since coming overseas).
			Lt Col Sir J L Harrington KCMG, KCVO, CB late CO of Battn & 20313 RSM Boden J mentioned in dispatch by Genl Sir Douglas Haig, GCB. Cr in Chief British Forces in France dated 30/4/16.
	15/06		Lt G H Walker transferred to R.F.C. 15/6/16.
			4 men wounded ('B' Coy).
			[d.o.w. Pte. 20549 George Dean]
	20/06		[d. Pte. 20147 Pte. Stanley Foreman]
	21/06		21469 Pte Roberts H 'B' Coy thro negligence caused Self Inflicted Wound & tried by F.G.C.M.

Instructions for the Forward Communication Trench Parties.

1.   The O.C. 11th South Lancs will be responsible for seeing that the following parties required for this work are detailed and equipped as per margin*, and that they are at their place of assembly at 8 pm on "Y" day.

        *Each man to carry pick & shovel and 6 sandbags.

(a)   ½ Coy to open communication through trench from Sap A.P.3 to GERMAN WOOD STANLEY AVENUE).

(b)   1 Coy to open communication trench from Sap A.P.4 to enemy's trenches and onwards (MARICOURT AVENUE).

(c)   ½ Coy to open communication trench from Sap No.6 (A.9/3) (SUPPORT AVENUE) to enemy's trenches and onwards.

(d)   ½ Coy to open communication trench from Sap No.5 (A.9/4) (WEST AVENUE) to enemy's trenches and onwards.

2.   He will also see that the following instructions are communicated to the O.C. of each party.

(i)   All parties to move as follows:-

        (a) and (b) parties, the latter leading, to move up to our own front line trench via STANLEY AVENUE as soon as the supporting Battalion of 89th Infantry Brigade has left its Assembly trenches, the leading man to wheel to the left on arrival at our own front line trench. Both parties should then be opposite the Sap they are to deal with. They should move out to their objectives as soon as the Supporting Battalion has crossed the enemy's Support line trench.

        (c) and (d) parties, the latter leading, to move up to our front line trench via SUPPORT AVENUE as soon as the supporting Battalion of 21st Infantry Brigade has left its Assembly trenches, the leading man wheeling to the left on arrival at our front line trench. Both parties should move along the front line until opposite the saps they are to deal with. They should move out to their objectives as soon as the Supporting Battalion 21st Infantry Brigade, has crossed enemy's support line.

(ii)   Work on the communication trench to be made between the head of the Russian Saps and the enemy's first line to be commenced at both ends.

(iii)   On completion of these trenches each party is to prolong its trench into the enemy's lines along existing trenches as shown on the attached map[1]. The

------

[1] The map refered to was not available to reproduce here.

Officer in charge each party should reconnoitre the enemy's trench he is to deal with before his party complete their first task.

21st June 1916   Lieut-Col R.E.

Instructions for the Communication Trench Maintenance Parties

1.   The O.C. 11th South Lancs will detail the following parties equipped as per margin*, and see that they are properly distributed in their respective trenches on the commencement of operations; i.e. 8 am "U" day.

    *Each man a shovel, every 4th man a pick. Each Platoon to have 500 sandbags dumped at suitable points outside the Avenue.

    (a) 1 Platoon for maintenance of STANLEY and MARICOURT AVENUES.

    (b) 1 Platoon for maintenance of SUPPORT and WEST AVENUES.

2.   He will also be responsible for the collection of the following stores by "T" day at the places noted, these to be at the disposal and in charge of the parties noted in Para.1.

    (a) In NAPIER KEEP

1,000	sandbags.
10	rolls wire netting.
50	sheets expanded metal.
50	7' pickets.
100	long angle iron posts (if available).
2	coils plain wire.

    (b) In "U" Works

1,000	sandbags.
10	rolls wire netting.
50	sheets expanded metal.
50	7' pickets.
100	long angle iron posts (if available).
2	coils plain wire
3	pitprops
20	planks 9" x 3"

    These stores are to be provided from current issues from the Divisional dump.

3.   He will be responsible for explaining to all ranks of those parties that on no account are they to move along the trenches for which they are responsible, in the opposite direction to which the trenches are marked to be used. Should they have to move in the opposite direction, they must leave the trench and go across country.

Lieut-Col R.E.
C.R.E. 30th Divisional
(County Palatine) Engineers

21st June 1916.

Table of Dispositions of R.E's and Pioneers

1. STRONG POINTS PARTIES.

89th
Infantry
Brigade

(a) 1 Section 200th Field Co. R.E.
    1 Platoon Pioneers
    2 Platoons Infantry

Trenches in MARICOURT (N) (East Face and part of South Face of CHATEAU KEEP - 140x of trench).
To prepare "Strong Points" at A.10.d.1.6 and A.10.a.4.6.

21st
Infantry
Brigade

(b) 1 Section 202nd Field Co. R.E.
    1 Platoon Pioneers
    1 Platoon Infantry

Assembly trench x x.
To prepare "Strong Points" at A.3.d.6.2.

90th
Infantry
Brigade

(c) 201st Field Co. R.E.
    1 Platoon Infantry

Copse Valley.
Defence of MONTAUBAN Village.

2. COMMUNICATION TRENCH PARTIES.

Division.

(a) ½ Coy. Pioneers.

Trenches in MARICOURT (S). (East Face of NAPIER KEEP - 300x of trench).
To open Communication Trench from Sap A.P.3 to GERMAN WOOD (STANLEY AVENUE).

(b) 1 Coy. Pioneers

-ditto-
To open Communication Trench from Sap A.P.4 to enemy's trenches and onwards. (WARICOURT AVENUE).

(c) ½ Coy. Pioneers.

"U" Works North of PERONNE Road.
To open Communication Trench from Sap No.6 (A/9/3) (SUPPORT AVENUE) to enemy's trenches and onwards.

3.   ROAD PARTIES.

Division.   (a) 1 Section 200th Field Coy. R.E.
                  ½ Coy. Pioneers.

            (b) 2 Sections 238th A.T.Coy. R.E.

            MARICOURT Trenches. (South Face of NAPIER KEEP - 200x
            of trench).
            Roads and bridges North of PERONNE Road.

4.   TRENCH MAINTENANCE PARTIES.

            (a) 1 Platoon Pioneers.

            STANLEY & MARICOURT AVENUES.
            Maintenance STANLEY & MARICOURT AVENUES.

            (b) 1 Platoon Pioneers.

            SUPPORT & WEST AVENUES.
            Maintenance SUPPORT & WEST AVENUES.

5.   DIVISIONAL RESERVE.

            200th Field Coy. (less 2 secs).*

            Copse Valley.

            202nd Field Coy. (less 1 sec.)

            Copse Valley

            2 Platoon Pioneers.

            Copse Valley.

            * 1 sect to move up to MERSEY ST at 2 hrs then to be under
            orders of 89th Bde.

STRONG POINT PARTY - 21st Infantry Brigade

Party.   1 Section 202nd Field Co. R.E.   32 men)
         1 Platoon Pioneers   40 men) R.E. Officer in charge.
         1 Platoon Infantry (Carriers)   40 men)

                                   Carried by
Stores. 20 coils barbed wire   20 Infy.
         50 short pickets   10 Infy.
         300 sandbags   10 Infy.
         448 sandbags   (4 each Sapper and Pioneer
                                    (and 40 Infantry.

         Guncotton 10-lb. 2 charges.

Tools. Sappers (6 hand axes or billhooks.
                  (2 saws.
                  (2 crowbars.
                  (6 prs. Wirecutters.
                  (2 hammers and 5" nails.
                  (2 mauls.
                  (remainder pick and shovel.

         Pioneers - Each man pick and shovel.

                                        Lieut-Col R.E.
                              C.R.E. 30th Divisional
21st June 1916.   (County Palatine) Engineers

STRONG POINT PARTY - 89th Infantry Brigade

Party.   1 Section 200th Field Co. R.E.   32 men)
           1 Platoon Pioneers   40 men) R.E. Officer in charge.
           1 Platoon Infantry   40 men)

                                            Carried by
Stores.   20 coils barbed wire   20 Infy.
          50 short pickets   10 Infy.
          300 sandbags   10 Infy.
          448 sandbags   (4 each Sapper and Pioneer
                                        (and 40 Infantry.

          Guncotton 10-lb. 2 charges.

Tools.   Sappers   (6 hand axes or billhooks.
                      (2 saws.
                      (2 crowbars.
                      (6 prs. Wirecutters.
                      (2 hammers and 5" nails.
                      (2 mauls.
                      (remainder pick and shovel.

          Pioneers: Each man pick and shovel.
          Infantry: 40 men - each man pick and shovel.

  Lieut-Col R.E.

                                         C.R.E. 30th Divisional
21st June 1916.   (County Palatine) Engineers

[30th Division C.R.E. War Diary]

Place	Date	Hour	Summary of Events and Information
	22/06		1 man 'B' Coy killed.
			[k.i.a. Pte 20356 Arthur Stubbs]
	23/06		Battn left for Bray & Etinehem. 'C' & 'D' Coys to former place 'A' 'B' & HQ to latter.
			1 man 'A' Coy killed.
			[k.i.a. Pte. 20572 Joseph Richardson]
Etinehem	01/06 23/06		H.Q. R.E. were at ETINEHEM with Divisional H.Q. During this period a considerable amount of work was carried out by Field Companies and the Pioneer Battalion under C.R.E.'s direction. It consisted almost entirely of preparing the Divisional Front for active operations by the construction of additional communication trenches, shelters, assembly places, dressing stations, Battle H.Q. &c. During the last week of this period assistance was given by 1½ Field Companies and Pioneers of the 9th Division. By the 23rd the Division's Battle Front was complete in all essentials. [30th Division C.R.E. War Diary]
	26/06		'A' 'B' & HQ move to BRAY.
			1 man 'C' Coy killed 1 NCO wounded 1 man Shell Shock.
			Work during month June 1916 chiefly on Trenches & preparing for British Advance originally fix for June 25 1916 but postponed to 1st July.
			[k.i.a. Pte. 20967 Edward Hill]

WATER TRUCK PARTY

The O.C. 11th South Lancs. will be responsible for detailing the following party for working the water trucks from CARNOY and TALUS BOISE forward:-

> 1 Officer - Lieut. CULSHAW 11th S.Lancs.
> 6 men
> (10 men already detailed by 21st Infantry Brigade for duty with 202nd Field Co. R.E.)

2. The Officer i/c Party will take over 4 water trucks each carrying a 400 gallon tank from the 202nd Field Co. R.E. on the 26th June and arrange at once in direct communication with Lieut. Beattie R.E. 92nd Field Co. R.E. (18th Division) for filling all tanks at TALUS BOISE as well as the tanks on the trucks by night Y/Z.

3. The party under O.C. 202nd Field Co. R.E. (1 sapper fitter and 4 Infantry) will be at the disposal of the Officer i/c water trucks for this purpose.

4. Arrangements have been made with the 18th Division for the construction of a siding at TALUS BOISE sufficient to take the water trucks of both Divisions.

Sd. R.G.Stene Capt. R.E.
for Lieut.Col. R.E.
C.R.E. 30th Division
(County Palatine) Engineers

26.6.16

[30th Division C.R.E. War Diary]

PRELIMINARY ORDERS

'A' CO.

No 3 party will consist of 2 platoons of 'A' Coy under Capt Champion.

No 4 party   ditto   ditto   ditto   under 2nd Lt. A.D. Walker.

Both parties will assemble in "U" works North of Peronne Road on a day to be fixed later.

No 3 Party will open up Communication trench from Sap No 6 (A 9/3) at head of Support Avenue to enemy's trenches and onwards into enemy's lines.

No 4 Party will open communication trench from Sap No 5 (A 9/4) (West Avenue) to enemy's trenches and onwards.

Both parties No 4 leading will move up SUPPORT AVENUE to our first line trench as soon as the supporting battn of 21st Infy Brigade has left its assembly trenches. On reaching the front line the leading man will wheel to the left. Both parties will move along the front trench until opposite their respective saps. They will leave the front line trench over the top and get to work simultaneously on both ends of the communication trench as soon as the supporting battalion 21st Infy Brigade has crossed enemy's support line.

On completion of these trenches each party is to prolong its trench into enemy's lines along existing trenches.

O.C. each party will reconnoitre enemy's trenches he has to deal with while the party is completing its final task.

Each man will carry a pick and shovel and 6 Sandbags.

O.C. 'A' Coy is responsible that all Officers & sergeants under his command thoroughly understand what their parties have to do, and that they study the ground and the map of the enemy's trenches beforehand.

He will also be responsible for getting in touch with the supporting Battn 21st Infantry brigade.

Detailed orders will be issued later.

Place	Date	Hour	Summary of Events and Information
	29/06		[d.o.w. Pte. 20999 William Keogh]
	30/06		Battn assembled in Trenches at various fixed points by 7-30pm 30/6/16.

1 man 'D' Coy self inflicted wound - shot himself thro' finger about 1 hour prior to Coy moving up to Trenches. To be tried by F.G.C.M.

Battn Headquarters changed to COPSE RAVINE evening of the 30th June, 19116. All parties in position by 7.25 p.m. viz.

1. 'A' Coy 2 Platoons assembld in "U" Works N of Peronne Rd.

2. 'A' Coy 2 Platoons assembld in "U" Works N of Peronne Rd.

3. 'B' Coy 2 Platoons assembld in Trenches in MARICOURT(S) East Face of NAPIER KEEP (300x of trench

4. 'B' Coy 2 Platoons assembld in COPSE VALLEY as Divisional Reserve.

5. 'C' Coy 4 Platoons assembld in Trenches in MARICOURT(S) (East Face of NAPIER KEEP as Divisional Reserve.

6. 'D' Coy 1 Platoon assembld in Trenches in MARICOURT(S) (East face & part of South Face of CHATEAU KEEP (140x of Trench)

7. 'D' Coy 1 Platoon assembld in DIXONS DITCH Trench.

8. 'D' Coy 1 Platoon assembld in STANLEY & MARICOURT AVENUES. (Maintenance Parties)

9. 'D' Coy 1 Platoon assembld in SUPPORT & WEST AVENUES. (Maintenance Parties)

1. Objective. To open Communication Trench From Sap No 6 (A/9/3) Support Aven)

Place	Date	Hour	Summary of Events and Information

2. Objective. To open Communication Trench From Sap No 5 (A/9/4) West Aven)

3. Objective. To open Communication Trench From Sap No 3 to German Wood (Stanley Aven)

4. Objective. Divisional Reserve.

5. Objective. To open Communication Trench from Sap A.P. 4 to enemy's trenches & onwards (Maricourt Aven)

6. Objective. Prepare Strong Points at A 10 d 1/6 & A 10 a 4/6

7. Objective. Prepare Strong Points at A 3 d 6/2.

8 & 9. Maintenance of Communication Trenches and opening of Russian Saps on evening of 1.7.16

Lewis Gun Section assembled in "U" Works on the 30th June and did not move during operation.

01/07 — The Battalion took part in the Offensive carried out by the 30th Division on the right of the British front. Hour of Zero 7.30 a.m. 1st July, 1916.

The duties and objectives allotted to the Battalion as above were carried out to time.

At 2.45 p.m. on 1st July 2 Communication Trenches were through to German front Line to a depth of 4 feet. (Nos 2 and 4 from right of sector) At 3.43 p.m. No 1 Communtn Trench was open to a depth of 4 feet. All these 3 were immediately continued and work progressed favourably.

No 3 was not ready till much later owing to heavy casualties from Shell fire. At 9.20 p.m. Russian Saps were opened by Trench Communication Parties. Saps from A.P. 3 & 4

Place	Date	Hour	Summary of Events and Information
			and A.P. 5 & 6.

Parties also provided on MONTAUBAN - MARICOURT ROAD.

[d.o.w. L/Cpl. 20087 Bertrand Allander; k.i.a. Pte. 21240 Thomas Beckett, Pte. 20057 William Bryan, L/Cpl. 20804 William Cotterill, Pte. 21352 William Davies, Pte. 20628 Albert Edwards, Lt. Reginald Garton, Pte. 20168 James Hodgins, Pte. 21378 Thomas Houghton, Sjt. 20070 Thomas Jackson, Pte. 21779 Patrick Kelly, Pt 20629 Thomas Kelly, Pte. 20121 Thomas Kinsey, Pte. 21367 James McDonald, Pte. 21803 Thomas Montgomery, Pte. 21473 James Mullen, Pte. 21054 William Oakes, Pte. 21316 Francis Ovens, Pte. 20415 George Parr, Pte. 21909 John Skelhorn, Sjt. 21879 John Small]

Place	Date	Hour	Summary of Events and Information
	02/07	14:00 16:00	O.C. Sap working party reported the Saps A.P. 5 and A.P. 6 were uncovered by 2-5 p.m.
		17:00	At Sap A.P. 6 the sap fell in a great deal and so caused the trench to be rather wider than it ought to be.

Owing to the bad state of trench East side of MARICOURT-BRIQUETERIE road in the old German lines the communication trench was fixed from A.P. 3 to run via strong point 1/89 along east side of GERMANS WOOD to CASEMENT TRENCH.

Place	Date	Hour	Summary of Events and Information
		19:25	Communication trench from No 5 Sap A 9/4 is now usable up to strong point 4/21.

Communication trench from Sap No 6 A 9/3 usable to strong point 1/21.

Place	Date	Hour	Summary of Events and Information
		19:30	Communication trench from A.P. 4 via strong points 2/89 through to strong point 2/2 in DUBLIN TRENCH.

[d.o.w. Pte. 21862 William Gibbons, Cpl. 20402 Harry Preston;

Place	Date	Hour	Summary of Events and Information
			k.i.a. L/Cpl. 20531 William Mustard]
Dugouts near Bray	02/07		During the night the 9th Division relieved the parties of 11th S. Lancs. on two of the main communication trench extensions. Work on the other two and also on the MARICOURT - MONTAUBAN road was continued. O.C. 11th S. Lancs. reported at 9.20pm that all four main communication trenches were usable for 500 yards beyond old German front line. [30th Division C.R.E. War Diary]
	03/07		Officer i/c Strong Points 1/89 and 2/89 reported work still continues on Strong Points 1/89 and 2/ Strong Point 1/89 was heavily shelled on night of 2nd and work was therefore impossible. On examination later it was found that through shelling much damage has been done especially to face work. Shelling still continued at 11.30 a.m. when work on top is attempted particularly.
			By 3 p.m. all was clear from Sap A.P. 4 and good useable trench through to DUBLIN TRENCH.
			On the 1st July when our Parties followed the Infantry over the parapet many casualties were caused through the Division on the left being held up. Quite a number of them were caused through Machine Gun fire from the enemy.
			[d.o.w. Pte. 21156 William Stanton; k.i.a. Pte. 21175 Robert Jackson]

Account of R.E, operations from morning 1st July to Mid-day 2nd July, 1916.

11th Bn. South Lancs. Rgt. (Pioneers)

At the commencement of operations 1 Platoon was attached to 200th Field Co. R.E. Strong Point party, and 1 Platoon to 202nd Field Co. R.E. Strong Point party. Two and a half Companies divided into four parties were in readiness to make 4 forward communication trenches in continuation of our existing ones. Two platoons were engaged in maintenance of our 4 main communication trenches and two Platoons were in Divisional Reserve in COPSE VALLEY.

The four parties detailed for forward communication trenches started work about 8.30 a.m. (exact time not reported). At 2.48 p.m. the continuations of MARICOURT and WEST AVENUES by Nos. 2 and 4 parties had been completed to a depth of 4 ft. up to German front line, and at 3.23 p.m. it was reported that the continuation of STANLEY AVENUE by No.1 party had been completed to a depth of 5 ft up to German front line. Work on the continuation of SUPPORT AVENUE by No.3 party had been held up by heavy shelling and the party had suffered heavy casualties. At 6.18 p.m. No.1 party reported trench completed up to Strong Point 1/89 and were starting work on the continuation of CASEMENT TRENCH. At 9.22 p.m. No.4 party reported that they had practically finished trench up to German front line and at 9.31 p.m. a similar report was received from No.2 party.

At 8.45 p.m. instructions were sent to O.C. 11th South Lancs to send up 1 Platoon in Divisional Reserve to assist in work on the MARICOURT – MONTAUBAN road.

At 9.20 p.m. instructions were sent for the remaining Platoon in Divisional Reserve to commence opening Russian Saps continuing to STANLEY and MARICOURT AVENUE.

O.C. 11th South Lancs reported at 10.42 p.m. that he had already arranged for his original trench maintenance parties to carry out this work, and that it was in progress. He was consequently directed to employ the reserve Platoon to open the Russian Saps continuing WEST and SUPPORT AVENUES.

At 11.20 p.m. the O.C. 11th South Lancs was directed to withdraw his communication trench parties for rest and to continue work the following morning.

Lt.Col., R.E.

C.R.E. 30th Divl. (C.P.) Engrs.

3.7.16.

[30th Division C.R.E. War Diary]

Place	Date	Hour	Summary of Events and Information

CASUALTIES from 12 Noon 24/6/16 to 12 Noon 4/7/16

		Killed	Wounded	Missing	Total
11th South Lancs. Regt.	Officers	1	4	-	5
	O.R.	23	80	4	107
	Total	24	84	4	112

[30th Division A&Q War Diary]

Place	Date	Hour	Summary of Events and Information
	04/07		On the 4th instant the Battalion went back to rest in billets in the BOISE de TAILIES. On the 7th July 2 Coys were ordered back to the line to be under orders of 21st Brigade. 1 Coy at disposal of 2nd Bn Yorks Regt and other Coy remained in Reserve in Assembly Trenches. Work under orders of 21st Brigade who were to capture Southern end of TRONES WOOD and establish connection with a French attack. Result Coy with 2nd Yorks did very little work.
			Prior to this move however, viz 5th July 1916 2 Coys were employed on the preparatory work of cutting lanes from West to East through the Southern portion of BERNAFAY WOOD.
	08/07		Hd Qrs and 2 Coys moved up to COPSE VALLEY, the other 2 Coys joining on the 9 and 10th.
			Two Coys placed at the disposal of O.C. 21st Brigade to dig trenches and on road work.
			[d.ow. - Pte. 21329 Daniel Cunliffe; k.i.a. Pte. 21538 Walter Mullen]
	09/07		Disposition of Coys - 2 Coys working under direct orders of 21st Brigade and 2 Coys who went to Glatz Redoubt night of 8th and were not required, in COPSE VALLEY minus 1 platoon on Road work under 238th Coy R.E. Maricourt.
			[k.i.a. L/Cpl. 20985 Joseph Pike, Pte. 20606 John Trotter]

Place	Date	Hour	Summary of Events and Information
	09/07		Two Sections 201st Field Co. R.E. and another Coy. 11th South Lancs were ordered to move up to reinforce the Technical Troops with the Brigade.
			At 9p.m. 3 Sections 202nd Field Co. R.E. and 2 Sections 201st Field Co. R.E. with the 3 Coys. 11th South Lancs proceeded to dig and wire a trench from the S.E. corner of BERNAFAY WOOD and to fire-step and wire the SUNKEN ROAD (BRIQUETERIE - HARDICOURT) i.e. from S.29.e.3.2. to A.5.d.3.5. [30th Division C.R.E. War Diary]
	10/07		In the evening 3 Sections 200th Field Co. R.E., 2 Sections 201st Field Co. R.E. and 3 Coys. 11th South Lancs went up for work under arrangements made with the 90th Infy. Bde., who were relieved during the night 10th/11th by 89th Infy. Bde.
			Work done during the night:
			Trench from BERNAFAY WOOD to SUNKEN LANE completed and wired.
			Wire erected along SUNKEN LANE as far as CHIMPANZEE Trench by 201st Field Co. R.E.
			Support trench S. of TRONES WOOD, 130 yards traversed trench at Southern end dug to a depth of 3 feet.
			Trench to MALTZ HORN FARM, 120 yards at N. and deepened 1' 6". About 100 yards wire fence erected in front.
			All work rather interrupted by shelling.
			On completion of night's work all returned to COPSE VALLEY. [30th Division C.R.E. War Diary]

Place	Date	Hour	Summary of Events and Information
	10/07		[k.i.a. Pte. 20200 Ralph Kay, L/Cpl. 20786 Albert Roney, Pte. 20189 Charles Webster]
	11/07		In the evening 2 Sections 200th Field Co. R.E. 2 Sections 201st Field Co. R.E. and 3 Coys 11th South Lancs went up for work under 89th Infy. Bde.
			During the night there was a heavy counter attack on TRONES WOOD and all troops (including Technical units) were standing to. No R.E. work was possible.
			[30th Division C.R.E. War Diary]
	11/07		[d.o.w. Pte. 21682 George Owen; k.i.a. Pte. 21526 William Hanley]
	12/07		Battalion, less 1 Coy left at disposal of G.O.C. 18th Division for work on the BRIQUETERIE ROAD proceeded to GROVETOWN for rest.
			1 draft received of 7 Officers from 14th (S) Bn Worcester Regt.

CASUALTIES from 12 Noon 8.7.16 to 12 Noon 13.7.16

		Killed	Wounded	Missing	Total
11th South Lancs. Regt.	Officers	-	1	-	1
	O.R.	5	49	-	54
	Total	5	50	-	55

[30th Division A&Q War Diary]

Place	Date	Hour	Summary of Events and Information
	19/07		1 Coy under orders of G.O.C. 18th Division rejoined Battalion.
Happy Valley	20/07		Resting at GROVETOWN and moved to HAPPY VALLEY.
	21/07		Still in HAPPY VALLEY resting.
Talus Boise	22/07		Moved at night to TALUS BOISE Area in accordance with O.O. No 26, as Divisional

29

Place	Date	Hour	Summary of Events and Information
			Reserve, with an Officer representing the Battn at 21st Brigade and 89th Brigade Headquarters.
	23/07		No orders received from Brigades, therefore no work done.
			[d.o.w. Pte. 21454 Frederick Bowen]
	24/07		One Platoon worked on Div. Headquarters Dug-outs. Remainder of Battn worked on CABLE TRENCH from BRIQUETERIE to TRONES WOOD. Average depth 3 feet.
			[d.o.w. Pte. 20118 James Parr]
	25/07		One Platoon worked on Divl Headquarters Dugouts. CABLE TRENCH from Signal Station, BRIQUETERIE along North side of SUNKEN ROAD to BERNAFAY ALLEY dug. Cable Trench from TRONES WOOD to BRIQUETERIE dug to depth of 5 feet, except 300 yards dug only 3ft 6 inches.
	26/07		One Platoon worked on Divisional Headquarters Dugouts. Trench from GLATZ REDOUBT to SIGNAL STATION, BRIQUETERIE and on to SUNKEN ROAD dug. 300 yards of CABLE TRENCH from BRIQUETERIE to TRONES WOOD dug to an average depth of 5 ft. CABLE TRENCH along SUNKEN ROAD lengthened to A 5 d 76.96 dug.
			[d.o.w. Pte. 22006 Albert Haworth]
	27/07		One Platoon worked on Divl Headquarters Dugouts. 'C' Coy cut one track through TRONES WOOD 120 yards South of Railway. CABLE TRENCH from TRONES WOOD to BRIQUETERIE completed to depth of 6 feet and floor levelled. CABLE TRENCH along SUNKEN ROAD to A 5 d 76.96 deepened and levelled.
			[d.o.w. Pte. 20663 Peter Houghton]

Place	Date	Hour	Summary of Events and Information
	28/07		One Platoon worked on Divl Headquarters Dugouts. Trench between BERNAFAY WOOD & TRONES WOOD running N to S about 450 yards long dug. Average depth 4 feet. One Assembly Trench 4 feet deep 120 yards long dug on right of GUILLEMONT ROAD 200 yards E of TRONES WOOD. Reliefs working on Dugouts by BRIQUETERIE in Sunken Road. [k.i.a. C.S.M. 21037 Charles Norbury]
	29/07		One Platoon worked on Divisional Headquarters Dugouts. Two Assembly Trenches dug in front of N.E. side of TRONES WOOD. Average depth 3 ft 9 ins and a parapet of 2 ft. Both 120 yds long. One Assembly trench dug on the right of GUILLEMONT ROAD in front of TRONES WOOD. Average depth 4 ft 120 yards long. Four paths through TRONES WOOD finished and clearly defined with strips of Calico. Reliefs still working on dugouts near BRIQUETERIE in Sunken Road.
	30/07		Reliefs worked all day on dugouts near BRIQUETERIE in Sunken Road. 2 Officers as representatives of this Battalion reported, one to 89th Brigade and one to 90th Brigade Headquarters. Battn awaited orders for work in connection with O.O. No 28 dated 28th July 1916. [k.i.a. Pte. 20132 Peter Maloney]

BATTLE CASUALTIES 24th JUNE to 31st JULY 1916

		Killed	Wounded	Missing	Total
11th South Lancs. Regt.	Officers	1	11		12
	O.R.	29	164	4	197
	Total	30	175	4	209

[30th Division A&Q War Diary]

NOTE re WORK DONE BY TECHNICAL UNITS DURING THE PERIOD 20th - 29th JULY AND DURING THE OPERATIONS 29th - 30th JULY.

11th South Lancs

Cable trenches 3' deep were made from BRIQUETERIE to TRONES WOOD and to the West of Maltz Horn Farm trench.

COBHAM trench was completed and the trench leading to the Dug Outs in the BRIQUETERIE was also completed in order to provide communication to the Dugouts.

Four Assembly trenches each 120 yards long were dug to a depth of 3' 9" (average) on the East side of TRONES WOOD.

An assembly trench between TRONES and BERNAFAY WOODS was extended South for 450 yards and dug to a depth of 3' 9" (average).

Four Rides were cleared through TRONES WOOD and marked with strips of calico.

One platoon worked with the 202nd Field Co. R.E. on Divisional Headquarters Dug Outs near BILLON FARM.

<table>
<tr><td></td><td>Lt-Col. R.E.</td></tr>
<tr><td>1st August 1916.</td><td>C.R.E. 30th Division</td></tr>
</table>

[30th Division C.R.E. War Diary]

Place	Date	Hour	Summary of Events and Information
Happy Valley	01/08		Battn resting in HAPPY VALLEY after the previous months operations. Casualties during operations of July 1916 amounting to 190 Other Ranks.
Hallencourt	02/08		Battn away from Fighting Area to Rest in Back Area viz HALLENCOURT. Entrained at MERICOURT STN for LONGPRE. Arrived late at night and marched to HALLENCOURT arriving there about 2-30 a.m. on the 3.8.16.
	03/08		Received orders that we should move on the 4th instant.
	04/08		Battn left HALLENCOURT for PONT REMY Station and thence by rail to MERVILLE.
			Battn arrived at MERVILLE Station had to march back to MOLINGHEM arriving about 11-30 p.m.
	10/08		Remained at MOLINGHEM until 10th instant when Battn moved at 4 a.m. in the morning en route for GORRE, where we arrived about noon after a 15 miles march.
	11/08 to 13/08		Utilised by men for cleaning up generally.
	14/08		Battn started work in new area viz FESTUBERT & GIVENCHY areas.
			'A' Coy right sector of line under 202nd Field Coy. R.E.
			'B' Coy left sector of line under 200th Field Coy. R.E.
			'C' Coy village line under O.C. 201st Field Coy R.E. 'D' Coy on Drainage of the 30th Divisional Area.
			[d.o.w. Pte. 21696 Albert Tickle]

Place	Date	Hour	Summary of Events and Information
	15/08		'A' Coy had 4 Casualties on the 1st day in the line (Wounded).
			'A' Coy had 2 more casualties wounded.
			'B' Coy had 1 Killed & 5 Wounded.
			[k.i.a. Pte. 20336 Thomas Naylor]
	16/08		Marched to ACQ about 1 mile and stayed there the day.
Cambligneuil	17/08		Left ACQ and marched to CAMBLIGNEUIL.
	19/08		Left CAMBLIGNEUIL and marched to SAUT Station and entrained for DOULLENS and re-joined the 30th Division. Marched from DOULLENS to LONGUEVILLETTE.
	22/08		Coys doing Coy Drill and general training.
			2 Men of 'A' Coy wounded.
	24/08		The General Officer Commanding, First Army, presented on the 24th instant, on parade, the riband of the Military Medal awarded to No 20089 Pte J. FRODSHAM of this Battn 'A' Coy for gallantry and devotion to duty.
	27/08		Battalion left 30th Division, and moved to 15th Corps area by Busses (DERNANCOURT).
	28/08		5 Officers joined Battn ex 1/3rd Monmouth Regt (T.F.)
	31/08		Strength of Battn on the 31st August 1916 Other Ranks 887. (Actually with Bn).
Bethune	12/08 to 31/08		During the month normal maintenance work was carried out in the line and calls for no special comment.
			To each Field Company was attached 1 Company 11th South Lancs (Pioneers) for work. The fourth Company 11th South Lancs was employed on drainage. The Divisional R.E. Dump was established at GORRE BREWERY, this site being more convenient

Place	Date	Hour	Summary of Events and Information
			than LE TOURET where that of the 39th Division had been situated. [30th Division C.R.E. War Diary]
	01/09		Battalion still in the FESTUBERT & GIVENCHY Sectors as per Report of last month.
			Battalion billetted in GORRE.
	03/09		[d.o.w. L/Cpl. 20028 James Large; k.i.a. Pte. 22106 John Plumpton]
	06/09		Received a draft of 16 O. Ranks.
	09/09		Received very urgent orders to be prepared to Move to 17th Corps Area at 1 hours notice.
			However did not move off until 6 p.m. on the 10th, and marched to BETHUNE Station and there entrained for AUBIGNY Station, and afterwards marched to ECQUVRES arriving there in the ear hours of the morning on the 10th.
Bethune	10/09		On 10th instant the 11th South Lancs (Pioneer Battalion) received orders to leave the Division for work under 17th Corps, and on the 12th instant the 200th Field Co. R.E. received similar orders. This necessitated a change in the distribution of the 2 remaining Field Companies.
			The 201st Field Co. R.E. took over the FESTUBERT Section.
			The 202nd Field Co. R.E. continued work in the GIVENCHY Section.
			The Drainage work which had been under the 11th South Lancs was continued by a party of 50 R.A.M.C. and 6 Sappers and remained in charge of the same officer of the 11th South Lancs who was retained for the purpose. [30th Division C.R.E. War Diary]

Place	Date	Hour	Summary of Events and Information
	11/09		Coys ordered to proceed to points as follows for work 'A' Coy to FORT GEORGE.
			'B' Coy to the EMPIRE & PYLONES.
			'C' & 'D' Coys to NEUVILLE ST VAAST.
	15/09		Received a draft of 1 Officer (Q.M.) and 4 O. ranks.
			Received urgent orders to again move.
	19/09		Left CAMBLIGNEUIL and marched to SAVY Station and entrained for DOULLENS and re-joined the 30th Division. Marched from DOULLENS to LONGUEVILLETTE.
	21/09		Left LONGUEVILLETTE and marched to HAVERNAC where the whole of the 30th Division were round about resting.
	22/09 25/09		Coys doing Coy drill and general training.
	27/09		Battalion left 30th Division, and moved to 15th Corps area by busses (DERNANCOURT).
Vignacourt	21/09 to 30/09		Moved by road to VIGNACOURT where Divisional H.Q. was established. The Division was engaged in a short course of training during this period. The Field Companies unfortunately, were not given the opportunity to benefit much by this as they were ordered, together with 11th South Lancs, to join the 15th Corps on the 27th instant. They were employed under 15th Corps on road repairs between MONTAUBAN and BAZENTIN. [30th Division C.R.E. War Diary]
	28/09		Battalion marched from DERNANCOURT to MONTAUBAN. The Germans evidently having noticed the Tents being erected by means of his Observation Balloon shelled during the night in the vicinity. Struck camp at 6 a.m. next morning and moved to various

Place	Date	Hour	Summary of Events and Information
			shelters in trenches.
			1 man wounded of 'A' Coy.
	30/09		Time during the month taken up chiefly with preparing to move and actually moving.
			Received a letter of congratulations from G.O.C. XVII Corps on the work done by the Battalion during the short stay with them.
			Battalion about 69 Other Ranks under strength on the 30th and 14 Officers under strength.
Montauban	01/10		Battn at MONTAUBAN under orders of 41st Division, for work on roads, at BAZENTIN.
			[k.i.a. Pte. 20381 William Kenny]
	03/10		2 Coys laying Duckboards in Fish Alley & Goose Alley, in forward area (Map ref M 30 a 6.4. & M 36 B 5.4.)
	05/10		[d.o.w. Pte. 21633 John Creaghan; k.i.a. Pte. 22382 Arthur Meek]
	08/10		2 Coys on road work, 3 platoons on night work in GOOSE ALLEY (clearing obstructions) and 1 Platoon on TURK LANE. 3 Platoons clearing obstructions in portions of FISH ALLEY, working from ABBEY ROAD to the rear.
			[k.i.a. Pte. 21706 Frank Baldwin]
	09/10		Battalion ordered to move to a new area at BAZENTIN-le-GRAND, and on arriving there no suitable place to be found anywhere, other Battalions and Bde Hdqrs being there, consequently Battalion received orders to stay where it was prior to moving to Bazentin-le-Grand.
	10/10		Battalion under orders of 30th Division.
Fricourt Chateau	11/10 to 17/10		On the 11th October Headquarters R.E. moved with Division H.Q. to FRICOURT CHATEAU on taking over from the 41st

Place	Date	Hour	Summary of Events and Information
			Division a portion of the front between EAUCOURT L'ABBAYE and GUEUDECOURT. The Field Companies and 11th South Lancs (Pioneers) were all camped near MONTAUBAN. [30th Division C.R.E. War Diary]
	12/10	14:00	Battalion moved up to Assembly trench in 21st Bde area S.5.a.6.4. at 2 p.m. Also Advcd Bn Hdqrs.
		16:30	Coys left to assemble in trenches for work at 6 p.m. each party sending an Officer and some men ahead to reconnoitre the ground to be worked, in connection with the Offensive to be taken by 30t Division.
		18:50	Following position and distribution of Battn.
			Advcd Hdqrs at S 5 a 6.4. Lewis Gunners under 21st brigade at S 5 b 7.3. 2 Coys in Fish Alley at 25 c 6.9. 2 Coys in Goose Alley.
			Coys unable to go out to dig trenches as per Operation Order No 40 owing to unfavourable situation. Orders then received from C.R.E. 30th Div for Coys to work on FISH ALLEY, pioneer lane & GOOSE ALLEY, behind our old front line.
			'A' & 'C' Coys then carried out the following work. 2 Coys dug 400 yds of extension of Fish Alley to average depth of 4ft 6inches N 25 c 2.2. to N 25 c 6.9. and deepened 400 yds to a depth of 5' 6" M 36 b 5.6. to N 25 c 2.2.
			2 Platoons dug new trench 140 yds long and 6ft deep from end of GOOSE ALLEY M 24 b 6.6. to trench or strong point held by 17th Kings Liverpool Regt at M 24 b 7.8.
			Remaining 1½ Coys at S 5 a 6.4. with Advcd Headquarters.
	12/10		The 30th Division was ordered to attack on 12th October (two Brigade front).

Place	Date	Hour	Summary of Events and Information
			The 11th South Lancs (Pioneer Battalion) was retained in its place of assembly [CREST TRENCH] till late in the evening, it was then sent forward and was able to dig a continuation to FISH ALLEY (one of our main communication trenches Right Brigade) behind our original front line and also to dig a communication trench 140 yards long from the end of GOOSE ALLEY (a main communication trench Left Brigade) to a strong point which had been formed slightly in advance of our original front line. [30th Division C.R.E. War Diary]
	13/10	14:30	Orders sent out to Coys to return at once.
			Battalion ordered to go forward again for purposes of digging trench to front line.
			Disposition. Turk Lane from Goose Alley along Abbey Rd. Result 1232 yds dug 5 feet deep 2ft bottom 4 ft top from point M 30 a 5.7. Junct of Turk Lane & Goose Alley.
	14/10		'A' Coy and 2 Platoons of 'B' on night work on FISH ALLEY extending it so as to be clear of Factory Corner avoiding all German trenches where possible. (idea, to avoid the possibilities of enemy artillery knowing the exact range of their old trenches and consequently shelling them thinking that Infantry etc would use them for assembly)
			[d.o.w. 2/Lt. William Fletcher]
	15/10		2 Platoons 'B' Coy on night work clearing out FISH ALLEY.
			'D' Coy on night work clearing out and completing GOOSE ALLEY.
			Work done on night 14th/15th Digging and extending FISH ALLEY 250 yds (new dug) Clearing up trench - FERRET TCH - to ABBEY RD 400 yds average depth 5½ feet.

Place	Date	Hour	Summary of Events and Information
			Clearing and deepening GOOSE ALLEY for 450 yards.
	18/10		Division continue offensive. Battalion moved to forward area also advcd H.Qrs in CREST TRENCH. Result of operation. 500 yards fire trench traversed and dug Average depth 4' 3" from end of TURK LANE to approx M 17 d central, & Fire trench traversed dug from M 24 a 8.2. about 500 yds.
	18/10		Communication Trench Parties
			Assembly in CREST TRENCH 4.30pm.
			To move under orders of O.C. 11th South Lancs as soon as the situation admits of work being commenced.
			Officers from each party to make necessary reconnaissance.
			(a) 1 Coy. 11 South Lancs. Continuation of C.T. from M.24.b.9.8. due North to front line. Existing trench South of M.24.b.9.9. to be cleared.
			(b) 2½ Coys. 11th South Lancs. Continuation of TURK LANE from M.24.a.1.7. to front line at M.18.d.3.7. as shown on map. [30th Division C.R.E. War Diary]
	20/10		Battn Lewis Gunners ordered to report to 21st Bde Hdqrs and to be attached to one of their Battalions to assist in the Line.
	21/10		1 Coy on TURK LANE, cleared from Front Line to about 100 yards South of GOOSE ALLEY, Sump holes dug at about 20 yds interval and trench boards laid over sumps.
			1 Coy on TURK LANE - from Eaucourt L'ABBAYE RD to SUNKEN ROAD in M 35, cleared and sump holes dug.
			1 Coy on FISH ALLEY 450-500 yds of trench cleared and about 12 sump holes dug, starting

Place	Date	Hour	Summary of Events and Information
			from the FACTORY - EAUCOURT L'ABBAYE RD and going South. 1 Coy on FISH ALLEY 1000 yards line widened deepened and made passable for Stretchers average depth 5' 6".
			[d.o.w. 2/Lt. Edgar Parr; k.i.a. Pte. 21441 William Helsby, Pte. 21245 Thomas Hynes, L/Sjt. 20345 Samuel Martin, L/Cpl 20467 Thomas Tipton]
	22/10		Battalion left vicinity of MONTAUBAN (Map ref S 26 b 8.7.) for DERNANCOURT CAMP, N of Dernancourt.
			[k.i.a. Pte. 20161 Frank Hartley]
	24/10		Battalion returned on the 24th to vicinity of MONTAUBAN (Map ref S 26 b 5.5.) for work on railways under the R.C.E. 4
	25/10		Work continued on Railways until the 5th
	05/11		11.16 when Battalion rejoined 30th Div on the 6.11.16.
	06/11		11th Bn. South Lancs Regt. Arrived by bus from Fourth Army area and billeted at HUMBERCAMP. [30th Division A&Q War Diary]
	28/10		[d.o.w. L/Sjt. 20294 Robert Sutton]
	01/11		[d. Pte. 6323 William Brotherhood]
	06/11 to 09/11		Battalion arrived at HUMBERCOURT by Bus from TALMAS, and stayed in billets until the 9th, when Battalion marched out to forward area to take over work from Monmouths.
			Battalion distributed as follows:- 2 Ptns of 'A' Coy 'B' Coy and 'D' Coy billetted at BERLES-au-Bois. 2 Platoons of 'A' Coy, Qr.Mrs stores and Transport at LA CAUCHIE and 'C' Coy at BAILLEULVAL.
			O.C. responsible for the Defence of BERLES-

Place	Date	Hour	Summary of Events and Information
			au-BOIS in case of attack by the enemy, on and from the 9th inst, when Monmouths left the area.
	10/11		Work carried on as taken over from Monmouths viz., Divisional Line and Defences of Village of BERLES-au-BOIS with the exception of 2 Ptns of "A" Coy on Roads in La CAUCHIE area and "C" Coy on roads in BAILLEULVAL area.
			Work carried on for the month, with the exception of inter-Coy reliefs on various works and roads Only 3 Casualties occurred during the month of Novr. 1916 all of which were wounded.
			"Gas" used by us British on our Divisional front on the night of the 12th inst, but no ill effects felt far back as BERLES-au-BOIS. (about 1,800 yds from front line).
			The "GAS ALERT" has been in force on frequent occasions during the last few days, the wind being favourable for enemy discharge of "Gas".
Bavincourt	01/11 to 30/11		The 11th South Lancs (Pioneers) were employed mainly on work on Division Line, Village Dug-outs, and Roads. [30th Division C.R.E. War Diary]
	01/12		Battalion distributed as follows:- Bn. Hd.qrs. 'B' & 'D' Coys & ½ 'A' Coy at Berles-au-Bois. 'C' Coy at Grosville & Transport at La Cauchie.
			With the exception of Inter-Coy relieves during the month, work carried on, on the Divisional Line & roads as last month.
			Work commenced on a new Strong Point "Panets Post" & finished with the exception of a few minor details.
	09/12		[d.o.w. Sjt. 20072 Harold West]

Place	Date	Hour	Summary of Events and Information
	13/12		Owing to our Artillery Operations on the 13th Decr. 1916, men ordered to Bombardment Stations Berles from 10 a.m. to 3 p.m. on that date, in case the enemy should retaliate on the village.
	14/12		[k.i.a. L/Cpl. 22005 Herbert Molloy]
	19/12		[d.o.w. Pte. 20159 Walter Tierney]
	23/12		[k.i.a. L/Cpl. 20620 Peter Mills]
	24/12		Enemy artillery very active, trying apparently to find some Big Guns (Siege battery) in position behind Battn Headquarters and again on the 29th Decr. 1916, the enemy artillery shelled Berles heavily.
	25/12		The Battalion rested on Xmas day, no work being done.
Bavincourt	01/12 to 31/12		The 11th South Lancs (Pioneers) Battn. Was employed mainly on work in Division Line and Road work under VIIth Corps. Work in the Division Line consisted in improving the state of existing defences and the construction of dug-outs. A new work to link up our Division Line with the Division Line of the Division on our Left was put in hand and practically completed during the month. The Pioneer Battalion also provided, under C.R.E's orders, parties for work on certain main communication trenches, a portion of front line trenches and a new Battalion H.Q. in B.2 Sub-sector.

During the last few days of the month work was concentrated on assisting Brigades in the opening up of main communication trenches which had suffered severely from the bad weather.
[30th Division C.R.E. War Diary]

1917

Place	Date	Hour	Summary of Events and Information
	01/01		[d.o.w. Sjt. 21176 Edward Ashby]
In the Field Berles-au- Bois	08/01		Battn moved from Forward area to back area as follows-
			Battn Hd Qrs to LUCHEUX, 'A' Coy to LA FONTAINE Fme 'B' Coy Larbret, Bailleulmont 'C' Coy to LARBRET 'D' Coy to La Folie Fme.
			'A' Coy employed on Felling trees in LUCHEUX Forest & 'D' Coy on Huts under O.C. Field Coys.
			'B' & 'C' Coys working on Railway Embankment at Crinchon Valley & later employed on Railway Work.
			During month nothing to report other than above Coys employed on works as above.
	22/01		'A' Coy moved to forward area "AGNY" for work under CRE 30 Divn.
	23/01		Captain R.F.BURY, 11th Bn. South Lancashire Regiment, appointed D.A.A. & Q.M.G. vice Major A.E.S.CLARKE. [30th Division A&Q War Diary]
	26/01		[d. Pte. 21788 Frank Burns]
Lucheux	01/02		Disposition of Battalion. Bn. Hd. Qrs & Transport at LUCHEUX. 'D' Coy at La Folie Farm. 'B' 'C' Coys at LARBRET. 'A' Coy in forward area at AGNY.
	02/02		[k.i.a. Pte. 21145 George Roy]
Simencourt	04/02		Battalion (less 'A' Coy at AGNY) moved to SIMENCOURT by march route via HUMBERCOURT - COUTERELLE SAULTY - BAVINCOURT - GOUY.
	05/02		Battalion (less 'A' Coy at AGNY) moved from SIMENCOURT to forward area as follows:-

44

Place	Date	Hour	Summary of Events and Information
			'D' Coy to ACHICOURT, 'B' & 'C' Coys to DAINVILLE. Transport & Qr.Mr. Stores remained behind at SIMENCOURT, and later moved to MONCHIET (23rd Feby 1917)

11th (S) Bn. South Lancashire Regiment

PRELIMINARY OPERATION ORDERS.

The Battalion will be employed during the forthcoming offensive on work as shown below.

These orders are liable to alteration.

'A' Coy.   1 Platoon will be engaged on the upkeep of roads in the area to the rear of AGNY.

1 Platoon will be engaged on the upkeep of Communications Trenches.

1 Platoon will be engaged on the upkeep of the Decauville Track. M.8.b.8.2. to M.9.d.6

(The above mentioned work will begin at the same time as the preliminary bombardment.

1 Platoon will be engaged on the forward Tramways along the Sunken Road, near G.20.

'B' Coy.   2 Platoons will be engaged clearing forward roads.

2 Platoons will be in Reserve.

'C' Coy.   This Company will be in Reserve.

'D' Coy.   2 Platoons will dig forward Communication Trench from the Sap at about the junction of Trenches at G.7 and G.8 to the German Sap marked Y.6 on the 1/10,000 Map.

2 Platoons will dig a Trench from G.11 to the German Sap marked Y.11 on the 1/10,000 Map.

Full details of all the proposed work will be issued later.

In the meantime, Officers Commanding Co.'s will, as far as possible, detail Officers for their prospective work, so that they may have an opportunity of reconnoitering the work, and the best means of getting to it.

'D' Coy will probably be in Assembly Trenches South of AGNY.

Remainder of the Battalion will be in the Assembly Trenches in the rear of AGNY CHATEAU.

H F Fenn Lt.Colonel.

17th Feb.1917.   Comdg 11th S.Lancs.Regt. (Pioneers).

Place	Date	Hour	Summary of Events and Information
	19/02		[d. Pte. 21491 Henry Roughley]
	21/02		[d.o.w. Pte. 21825 John Simpson]
	27/02		'D' Coy moved from ACHICOURT to AGNY on 27th Feby 1917, the former village having passed to the 29th Division.
			Companies employed during the period under review on the construction of Dugouts in the Line. 10 Casualties during month (all wounded).
			Strength of Battalion on the 28th Feby 1917:- 43 Officers 908 Other Ranks.
	01/03 17/03		From the beginning of the month until March 17th 1917 the Battalion was engaged in preparing dugouts, First Aid Posts and Collecting Stations in the forward trenches in front of AGNY.
	09/03		[k.i.a. Pte. 22170 John O'Grady]
	18/03		First news of the enemy's retirement towards the COJEUL SWITCH LINE, which took place during the night, was received in the morning. All the work was immediately stopped and the Battn stood pending the arrival of fresh orders. These arrived at noon and 'A' & 'B' Coys went out from AGN to the ARRAS-BUCQUOY the AGNY-BUCQUOY and the Mercatel SWITCH ROADS to prepare them for guns and transport. These roads behind the old German Lines had in several places been blown up. Temporary tracks were made round these spots while the Craters were being filled in an on the ARRAS-BUCQUOY Road a very large concrete barrier which straddled it was removed.
			Several booby traps were discovered and rendered harmless. 'C' and 'B' Coys relieved 'A' & "B Coys during the night and the Battalion continued on the work in continuous shifts

Place	Date	Hour	Summary of Events and Information
			until the 22nd inst.
Blairville	22/03		Battalion marched to new Billeting area in BLAIRVILLE, which had been evacuated by the Germans. Before leaving they had blown up all buildings likely to provide shelter for our troops, but with the material strewn about the village the Battalion were soon able to provide accommodation for itself. Work was continued in making the roads passable for traffic where they have been blown up by the enemy.
			[d. Pte. 20290 Samuel Dalton]
Blairville	01/04		Battn. in Billets at BLAIRVILLE.

INSTRUCTIONS TO THE O.C. 11th SOUTH LANCS PIONEERS

1.   You will assemble your battalion as follows:

   H.Q. and 3 Coys in trenches at M.20.a.and.b. 1 Coy in trenches at S.1.d. and S.7.b.

   The whole to be at their places of assembly by midnight Z - ½

2.   You will detail the following parties:

   (a) One Company on preparing MESCATEL - NEUVILLE VITASSE - WANCOURT road for wheel traffic.

   (b) One Company on preparing HENIN - ST>MARTIN - HENINEL - WANCOURT road and HENI - N.27.b. - N.22.s. - WANCOURT road for wheel traffic.

3.   You will receive direct orders from me when to move parties out.

G.W. Dennison
Lieut-Col. R.E.
C.R.E. 30th Division

4/4/1917

[30th Division C.R.E. War Diary]

11th South Lancashire Regt. (Pioneers).

OPERATION ORDER

No 40

By Lt.Col. H.F.Fenn, D.S.O., Comdg.

INSTRUCTIONS FOR O.C. No1.ROAD PARTY.	The party will consist of 'C' Coy under the Command of Major G.F. Beal, and will assemble at Billets in BLAIRVILLE ready to move off at ¼ hours notice from 1 p.m. "Z" day.
OBJECTIVE	To open for Wheeled traffic the following roads:-
	(A) Road running from BOIRY BECQUERELLE at T.7.a.9.8 via Cross Roads at T.1.c.7.2. HENIN sur COJEUL, MARTIN sur COJEUL, HENINEL, WANCOURT.
	(B) HENIN – St.MARTIN – N.28.c.3.3. N.27.b.3.7. N.22.a.7.3. – WANCOURT Road.
	Should Road between N.28.c.3.5 & N.27.b.3.7. be in a bad condition O.C. 'C' Coy will use either the alternative roads at N.33.a.3.2. or N.32.d.5.1. to the road running approximately parallel to the HENIN-HENINEL Road.
	In the event of both roads requiring much work you will open a road through to WANCOURT first.
RECONNAISANCE.	O.C. 'C' Coy will detail 2 Officers and 4 Other Ranks to reconnoitre 'A' & 'B' Roads respectively. These Officers will report to Batt. Headquarters at 12 noon "Z" day and will move on receipt of orders.
	They will send a report on state of these roads to await arrival of 'C' Coy at T.7.a.9.8.
INSTRUCTIONS FOR O.C. No. 2 ROAD PARTY	The party will consist of 'D' Coy under the Command of Captain H.A.Hodges, and will assemble at Billets in BLAIRVILLE ready to move off at ¼ hours notice from 1 p.m. "Z" day.

OBJECTIVE	To open up road for Wheeled Traffic from MERCATEL through NEUVILLE VITASSE to WANCOURT.
	The 56th Divisional Pioneers will be working from N.19.c.1.8. as far as WANCOURT. It is probable that 'D' Coy will open the road from MERCATEL to this point first. 'D' Coy will then take over the road from WANCOURT back to junction with 56th Divisional Pioneers.
RECONNAISANCE.	O.C. 'D' Coy will detail 1 Officer and 2 Other Ranks to reconnoitre the road. The Officer will report (with 2 Other Ranks) at the Battn Headquarters at 12 noon "Z" Day and will move on receipt or orders. He will send a report on state of the road to await arrival of 'D' Company at M.28.d.7.6.
DIVISIONAL RESERVE.	'A' & 'B' Coys will be in Reserve, and will be held in readiness to move at one hour's notice, from BLAIRVILLE.
EQUIPMENT.	Each man will carry a shovel and every 4th man a pick. 6 Sandbags, 50 rounds of S.A.A., unconsumed portion of "Z" days ration, iron rations & Full Water Bottle. Waterproof Sheet and Haversack will be worn on pack straps.
TOOLS. To be Taken by each Coy.	4 Axes, 2 Cross Cut Saws, Wire Cutters (as many as possible), Notice Boards for Roads, Rope for moving trees, and 6 Heavy Hammers for breaking bricks or stone for roads.
R.E. STORES.	R.E. Stores are available at Field Coy dumps situated at S.12.a.1.7. and M.35.d.3.6.
REPORTS.	O.C. 'C' and 'D' Coys will report as soon as possible as to state of the roads. Progress will also be reported every 3 hours and when either of the roads are open for Wheeled traffic to WANCOURT.
ESTIMATED CASUALTIES.	Will be sent when the number exceeds fifty. In the case of any casualty occurring to an Officer, his name must be stated on the returns.

	Actual Casualty Return to be sent with full details, made up to midnight, if possible each day.
TIMING OF MESSAGES.	All messages must be accurately timed.
	O.C. each Coy will detail an Officer to report at Bn. Headquarters at 9 a.m. on "Z" day to synchronise watches.
SIGNALS.	Messages will be sent by runner, & cyclists will be detailed for this purpose.
BATTN. HEADQUARTERS	Battn Headquarters for the present will be at BLAIRVILLE.
MEDICAL.	Regimental Aid Post will be close the Bn. Headquarters. Advanced Dressing Station will be established at S.3.a.0.5. Collecting Stations will be at S.5.d.5.1. and M.35.s.2.8. Walking Wounded will be directed to the Corps Walking Wounded Collecting Station at M.8.b.8.6.
	Aid Posts will also be at approx the following places.
	M.34.c.7.5., M.34.d.9.4., M.35.d.3.8., M.35.d.4.7., S.4.c.9.2., S.5.d.7.5., S.6.b.9.2., T.1.a.1.3.

H F Fenn
Lieut.Colonel.
Comdg 11th S. Lancashire Regt. (Pioneers).

7.4.1917.

Place	Date	Hour	Summary of Events and Information
	08/04		From 1st April, 1917 to this date Battalion engaged on roads in vicinity of BOISLEUX St. MARC BOISLEUX au MONT BOIRY BECQUERELLE and ARRAS-BUCQUOY Rd, making them suitable for Lorry Traffic.
	09/04		Coys stand to and await orders to move on the most forward roads in connection with the offensive which commenced on this date.
			At 3 p.m. 'D' and 'C' Coys moved off from Camp to commence work on the roads which detailed to them through Operation Order issued on the 7th.
			'D' Coy cleared the MERCATEL - NEUVILLE VITASSE Road for Horse Traffic by 5 a.m. on the 10th. This road was used by lorries before dawn on the 11th.
			'C' Coy went out to open for wheeled traffic Road running from BOIRY BECQUERELLE at T.7.a.9.8 via Cross roads at T 1 c.7.2. HENIN sur COJEUL MARTIN sur COJEUL, HENINEL WANCOURT, but owing to the unfavourable situation reports received, this Company was unable to work as far as detailed above. They worked on the HENIN - ST.MARTIN Road, which was opened for Horse Transport by the morning of the 11th April.1917.
			The Arras-BAPAUME Road was reconnoitered and reported on.
	10/04	06:30	'A' Coy went out to work in relief of 'D' Coy and 'B' Coy in relief of 'C' Coy.
	10/04		Two companies of 11th South Lancs Pioneers were employed all day on opening up the MERCATEL - NEUVILLE VITASSE and HENIN - St MARTIN Roads being relieved in the evening by two other companies of the same battalion who worked on these roads all

Place	Date	Hour	Summary of Events and Information
			night. The MERCATEL - NEUVILLE VITASSE Road was open and used by motor lorries on night of 10th/11th. The HENIN - ST MARTIN Road was open for horse transport by morning of 11th. [30th Division C.R.E. War Diary]
	11/04		From morning of the 11th until the Battalion was relieved on the 12th work was carried on, on the forward roads. The work consisting chiefly in making the roads passable for Lorries.
	11/04		Two companies of the 11th South Lancs Pioneers were employed all day on repair of the FICHEUX - MERCATEL - NEUVILLE VITASSE and FICHEUX - BOISLEUX AU MONT - NOIRY BECQUERELLE - HENIN - ST MARTIN Roads which owing to the very bad weather and very heavy traffic were in a bad condition. These two companies were relieved by two other companies of the same battalion who worked on the above roads all night of 11th/12th. [30th Division C.R.E. War Diary]
	12/04		Two companies of the 11th South Lancs Pioneers (less two platoons) were employed in the morning on repair of roads in Divisional area East of FICHEUX.
			At 9 a.m. one section of 200th Field Co. R.E. and two platoons of 11th South Lancs Pioneers went out to construct three Strong Points in the Support line of the HINDENBURG Line. Strong Points were constructed by above parties at N.27.b.95.45 - N.28.c.45.64 - and N.28.d.25.40. [30th Division C.R.E. War Diary]
	12/04	17:00	The Battalion left BLAIRVILLE and marched to BASSEUX - BAILLEUMONT area.

Place	Date	Hour	Summary of Events and Information
	13/04 to 14/04		Moved back to St AMAND, arriving there about 2 p.m. At about 11-30 p.m. however, wire was received from the Division that XVIII Corps orders were that we should be lent to the VII Corps for work on roads, and that we were to march to BOISLEUX au Mont on the 14th. We arrived there about 3-30 p.m. on the 14th and the men finding there was no accommodation readily adapted themselves to the circumstances and speedily erected improvised shelters from material at hand.
	15/04		Coys went out to work on roads in vicinity of BOISLEUX St.Marc and HENIN.
	18/04		Received orders from Division that we were to rejoin them on the 19th inst in the vicinity of BEAURAINS.
	20/04		On the morning of the 20th Coys went out to work on roads in the HENIN St MARTIN HENINEL & NEUVILLE VITASSE areas.
	22/04		200th Field Co. R.E. and Pioneers were employed on roads and crossings of River COJEUL at HENINEL. [30th Division C.R.E. War Diary]
	23/04		The work set out for the Battn in the operations which began upon the morning of April 23rd consisted in making the forward roads passable for artillery and transport. Later in the day as the result of certain developments in the situation one and half companies were called out to hold positions in the Corps Defensive Line and two platoons formed a protective guard for a battery when the position of affairs appeared for a time to be precarious. 'C' Coy paraded at 4-30 a.m. and were working on HENIN ST MARTIN HENINSEL Rd towards CHERISY. They were working on this

Place	Date	Hour	Summary of Events and Information

road up to the outskirts of HENINEL at 6 a.m.

'B' Coy followed up two or three hours later with the intention of working on the other side of HENINEL towards CHERISY. Officers were sent forward to reconnoitre, but the situation throughout the morning appeared to be rather uncertain. The enemy shelled HENINEL very heavily and 'C' Coy were quite unable to work in that village. 'B' Coy found the road from HENINEL towards CHERISY also under very heavy fire. Consequently the two Coys collaborated on the road behind HENINEL and did much useful work, repairing it as far up as possible.

'A' Coy also encountered lively shelling on their road which ran northwards out of HENINEL Village. It was little more than a cart track; the Germans had dug into its bank before it had been used, a short while previously, as part of our front line. The Coy managed to make it passable for transport before they ceased work on it.

By the end of the afternoon 'C' & 'B' Coys reported that the HENIN-ST>MARTIN-HENINEL Road was open for Lorry traffic as far as the last named village. In the evening two platoons of 'D' Coy were sent out to endeavour to work beyond HENINEL towards CHERISY and arrived at the Reserve Line just as the Infantry were going over again. Here they remained for a short while and were just moving up to their task when, the O.C. of a battery requested their protection for his gun This was immediately given, one platoon digging themselves in 200yds in advance of the Battery and one in line with the guns. After a few hours when the situation had cleared up these two platoons proceeded to their original

Place	Date	Hour	Summary of Events and Information
			task and worked on the road between HENINEL and CHERISY.
			'B' and 'C' Coys had returned to camp and the men had just turned in when orders were received for a company to be sent to occupy two strong points in the Corps Defensive Line. The effort and extent of the German counter attack on the right seemed to be doubtful and was the cause of this request. 'B' Coy were speedily called out again and with two platoons of 'D' Coy were sent off w two Lewis guns to occupy the two strong points.
			Here the men remained until remained until relieved by the 90th Bde on the afternoon of the 24th.
			On the following days, the Battalion continued the work on the roads around HENINEL.
	23/04		About 6.30pm on 23-4-17 I [C.R.E.] was instructed by G.S.O.1 to send troops out and occupy the Corps Defence Line, this I did with six Platoons of the 11th South Lancs (Pioneers) who remained there until relieved by Infantry next day.
			The Pioneers were employed on roads except two Platoons on Divisional H.Q. [30th Division C.R.E. War Diary]
Neuville Vitasse	25/04		On the 25th the C.R.E's Headquarters moved with Advanced Divisional Headquarters to M.18.d.central near NEUVILLE VITASSE. These Headquarters had been constructed by 1 section of 202nd Field Co. with 1 section 200th Field Co. and 1 Platoon 11th South Lancs. helping. [30th Division C.R.E. War Diary]
	26/04		[k.i.a. Pte. 31248 Albert Bailey, Pte. 20047 Henry O'Reilly]
	28/04		Battalion entrained at ARRAS Station and

Place	Date	Hour	Summary of Events and Information
			moved by train to Station about 8 miles S of St.POL. Marched to present Billets in BEAUVOIS.
	29/04		The 11th South Lancs (Pioneers) did very important work on the roads under heavy shell-fire. The Officers of this Battalion also carried out some very useful road reconnaissance. The six Platoons which went out to occupy the Corps Defence Line on the night of 23-4-17 had already worked all day on roads but went out when called upon to defend the line with cheerfulness and without a murmur and worked on the line all night. [30th Division C.R.E. War Diary]
	01/05 to 31/05		At the beginning of the month the Battalion was at BEAUVOIS, near ST.POL. It was the first time for many months that the Battalion as a whole had been able to go into training and some useful work was done. On the 15th, a move was made to the adjoining village of OEUF. The Battalion did not stay here long, and, two days later it proceeded northwards by Bus staying on successive night at ST.HILAIRE, HAZEBROUCK and PATRICIA CAMP Nr. POPERINGHE. From here it marched on the 20th to PALACE CAMP, near DICKEBUSCH. On the following day work was begun under the Chief Engineer Xth Corps upon Corduroy roads and Light railways. On the nights of the 27th, 28th and 29th PALACE CAMP was shelled by the enemy. Upon the 30th Division coming into the area the Battalion rejoined it, and on the night of the 31st marched to the ECOLE, east of YPRES, where it took up its quarters.
	27/05		[k.i.a. Pte. 21154 Patrick Makinson]

Place	Date	Hour	Summary of Events and Information
	29/05		[k.i.a. L/Cpl. 20869 Alfred Foster]
	30/05		[d.o.w. Pte. 20965 John Potter]
	31/05		[d.o.w. Pte. 19047 Charles Webb]
Ypres	01/06 to 30/06		At the beginning of the month the Battalion occupied the ECOLE to the East of YPRES, where it had arrived upon the 31st May, 1917. Upon the night of the 3rd/4th June, 1917, the whole Battalion was engaged in constructing a new fire trench 700 yards long, sited a distance of approximately 500 yards ahead of the front line. The trench, which ran South East of the MENIN Road, was to be 3ft wide & 3 ft deep and it was arranged that the fire bays only should be dug, the traverses to be completed later.

The Battalion paraded 720 strong and the population of No Man's Land that night was increased by a wiring party furnished by the Field Coy R.E., and a covering party provided by the 2nd Bedfordshire Regt. and the 19th King's Liverpool Regt.

The first Company started on the work at 11.10 p.m. but the company on the right, which was considerably delayed in reaching its task did not begin much before midnight. Nevertheless by 1 o'clock the Coys had completed all the 77 fire bays together with the two strong points required. At that time the enemy was fairly quiet, orders were issued for the Coys to begin work on the traverses.

During the whole night the enemy had been shelling fairly heavily a similar trench constructed shortly before on the left, later in the night they either saw or suspected that we were continuing it further south, because there was considerable machine gun fire, all of which went high, while 50 o 60 Shrapnel & H.E. shells were sent over. However, the only

Place	Date	Hour	Summary of Events and Information

casualty on the work was one man wounded, and before the men were withdrawn at 2 a.m. 24 traverses had been completed and all the others were well under way.

When returning to the ECOLE the Battalion ran into a very heavy barrage of Gas shells which also covered the billets. Although Small Box Respirators were used two officers & 12 men were gassed and several others Killed and wounded.

The M.O. did not consider it advisable for the men to work during the next 24 hours as so many were suffering from the effects of the gas. Upon the night of the 6th, however, the fire trench was completed and a communication trench back to the original front line was dug. Congratulatory messages upon the fire trench were received from the Divisional General and the C.R.E.

Work on the following nights was continued on trenches and roads. Upon Z day of the Battle of MESSINES, the 30th Division being to the left of the attacking Army, this Battalion stood-to in anticipation of work being required upon the Divisional front.

The Battalion remained at the ECOLE until 13th. During that time it was every day very heavily shelled with Gas or H.E. and the larger portion of the heavy casualties suffered by the Battn were sustained in Billets.

On the night of the 13th the Battalion moved to the Railway Embankments Dugouts where it was hoped more rest for the men would be possible. This unhappily was not the case. Every day the quarters were shelled with Shrapnel and heavy calibre shells and between the 13th and 27th fifteen dugouts were smashed in. Gas shells also were sent over on

Place	Date	Hour	Summary of Events and Information

two nights.

Since the 13th one Company had occupied bivouacs & shelters near the CHATEAU SEGARD and on the 27th the remaining three companies moved to the same spot. This neighbourhood owing probably to the proximity of batteries soon developed signs of unhealthiness.

Meanwhile the Companies had been working on VINCE ST. WELLINGTON CRESCENT. ZILLEBEKE St & roads in the area which were under close observation by day and were invariably shelled at night.

Their most important task was the construction of 3 Assembly Trenches 2 since christened FENN Lane & RIDGE St, together with one Communication trench joining them up & running from RIT St to WELLINGTON Crescent. A Comm Tch was also dug joining up VINCE ST with GOUROCK Rd about 270 yds long & trench boarded.

During the month of June, 1917 the Battalion suffered a very large number of casualties 1 Officer being killed, 1 wounded and Died of Wounds later, and 3 Other Officers wounded, one of whom is still at duty. Other Ranks killed 17, Wounded 88, Wounded still duty 38. These figures do not include Gas cases or Shell Shock cases.

| | 30/06 | | The 11th Btn. South Lancs. Regt. (Pioneers) were employed throughout the month in digging assembly trenches, and in maintaining the roads in the Divisional Area. The latter entailed considerable labour as they were frequently damaged by shell fire.
[30th Division C.R.E. War Diary] |

89th Brigade B.541.

The Officer Commanding.

17th, 19th, 20th Battalion K.L.R.
2nd Bn. Bedfordshire Regt.
89th Machine Gun Company.
89th Trench Mortar Battery.

1. A new trench will be dug by 11th Bn. South Lancashire Regiment and 200th, 201st, and 202nd Field Companies R.E. on the night of June 3rd/4th, as shown on the attached sketch.

2. Covering parties will be provided at approximately the points shown on the sketch as follows :-

A and B,   by the 2nd Battalion Bedfordshire Regt.

C, D, E, & F.   by the 19th Battalion K.L.R.

Each covering party will consist of 1 Section and 1 Lewis gun.

They will be clear of the front line trench by 10 p.m. so as not to interfere with the march of the working parties.

3. A carrying party of 60 men will be detailed by the 20th Battalion K.L.R. They will rendezvous at I.18.c.3/7 at 10.30 p.m., marching via CHINA WALL and BOND STREET. Instructions as to the material they will carry will be issued direct to the Officer Commanding, 20th Battalion K.L.R., by the Officer Commanding, 200th Field Company R.E.

4. BOND STREET and VINCE STREET will be kept clear of all traffic between the hours of 8 p.m. and 10.45 p.m.

5. After this trench has been dug, it will be held by posts during the hours of darkness, commencing from the night of 4th/5th June. Posts should not be at a greater distance than 100 yards apart, and should consist of not less than 6 men.

The Left Battalion will be responsible for this trench from the MENIN road to the point at which it ceases about I.18.d.5/2.

The two posts, which will be dug South of this point at about I.18.d.45/10 and I.24.b.35/80, will be garrisoned by the Right Battalion.

Edward Lascelles

Captain
Brigade Major.
89th Infantry Brigade.

2/6/1917.

OPERATION ORDER No. 41.

by

Lieut.Colonel. H.F. Fenn, D.S.O.,

Comdg. 11th (S) Bn. South Lancashire Regt.(Pioneers).

2nd June, 1917.

1. INTENTION.	It is intended to dig a Fire Trench during the night 3rd/4th June, dimensions as per attached plan, from I.18.a.5.6., through I.18.a.8.0, I.18.d.3.8., I.18.d.45.50. to I.18.d.5.2. and 2 Posts at I.18.d.45.10 and I.24.b.35.80.
2. INFORMATION.	The trench will consist of a series of Firebays, 9 yards long with 4 yards traverses. Only the Fire Bays will be dug.
	The 201st Field Coy R.E. will tape out the trench.
	The 200th and 202nd Field Coy R.E. will erect wire in front of the trench at the same time. A covering party will be furnished by the Brigade in the line.
3. DISTRIBUTION.	Coys will work in the following order.
	'D' Coy will be on the left. 'A' Coy. 'B' Coy. 'C' Coy on the right.
	'D', 'A' & 'B' Coys will each dig 20 bays.
	'C' Coy will dig the remaining bays 12 to 17 in number, and 2 Posts.
	5 Officers per Company will be taken. 8 men will be detailed for each Bay and 12 for each Post. Each Bay will be in charge of a N.C.O.
4. RENDEZVOUS.	D Coy and 'A' Coy, 'D' Coy leading, will proceed up BOND ST. and on reaching Font Line will turn left i.e. North, until they come to the end of the Wood at I.18.c.3.7. where they will be met by an R.E. Officer. These Coys to be at Rendezvous at 10.45 p.m. sharp.
	'B' Coy and 'C' Coy, 'B' Coy leading, will proceed up VINCE ST. and LOVERS WALK and will meet an R.E. Officer at I.18.d.3.1. at 10.45 p.m. sharp.

O.C. Coys will detail an Officer each, to be at Bn.Hd.Qrs ECOLE at 7 p.m. These Officers will act later as guides.

Should O.C. 'C' Coy find that he has more men than is necessary owing to the number of Bays being less than surmised, he will withdraw them to the Front Line near Lovers Walk, and at once report to Bn.Hd.Qrs.

Coy Cdrs will arrange to have at least 2 Coy runners with them.

In the event of work not being completed before, all parties will withdraw at 2 a.m.

5. BATTN. HDQRS.	Battn Headquarters will be at I.18.c.3.7. from 9 p.m.
6. MEDICAL.	4 Stretcher bearers and 2 stretchers will go with each Coy.

The Medical Officer and 4 H.Qrs. stretcher bearers will be at I.18.c.3.7.

7. RESERVES. There will be a reserve consisting of 1 N.C.O. and 10 men per Coy under 2nd Lieut. W.Ridsdale.

Coys will report as soon as possible if they are unable to turn out a sufficient number of men for this purpose.

8. DRESS. Coys will parade in Shirt Sleeves, and will carry Rifle, and Bayonet in Scabard, bandolier, box Respirators, 1 shovel and 15 Sandbags. Every 4th man will carry a Pick.

Sandbags to be drawn from Battalion dump.

9. REPORTS. Coys will report :

1. When their men commence work.
2. Progress at 1 a.m.
3. When work is completed.

10. ENEMY ACTION. If the enemy open Machine Gun or Artillery fire on any Company, it will take cover near the work.

No Coy is to leave work unless in the opinion of Coy Commander it is urgently necessary and there is no time to await orders.

In that case he will withdraw Coy into trenches, report and await orders.

Coys not immediately affected by hostile fire will continue work although other Coys may have had to withdraw.

| 11. COMPLETION OF WORK. | When BAY is complete the N.C.O. in charge will report To an Officer who will inspect it. If satisfactory the party will return to camp. |

H F Fenn
Lieut.Colonel.

2nd June, 1917.

Comdg.11th S.Lancs Regt. (Pioneers).

	Digging	SBs	Runners	CSM	Reserve	Total
A Coy	160	4	2	1	11	178
B Coy	160	4	2	1	11	178
C Coy	160	4	2	1	11	178
D Coy	160	4	2	1	11	178
	640	16	8	4	44	712

Plus 4 Orderlies }
2 Stretcher Bearers } 8 = 720
3/6/17 24 Officers 2 MOs Assts }

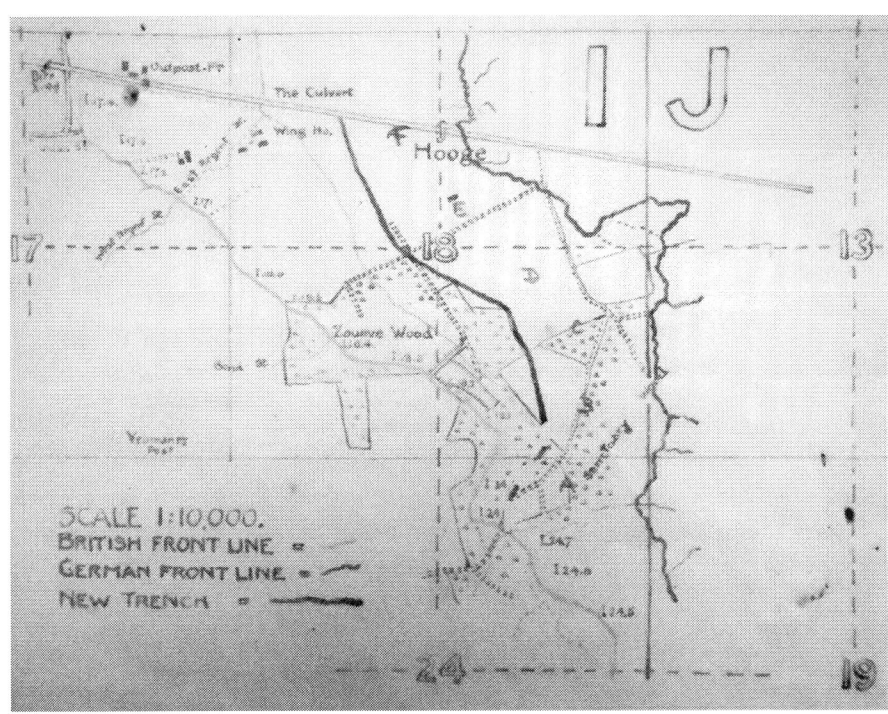

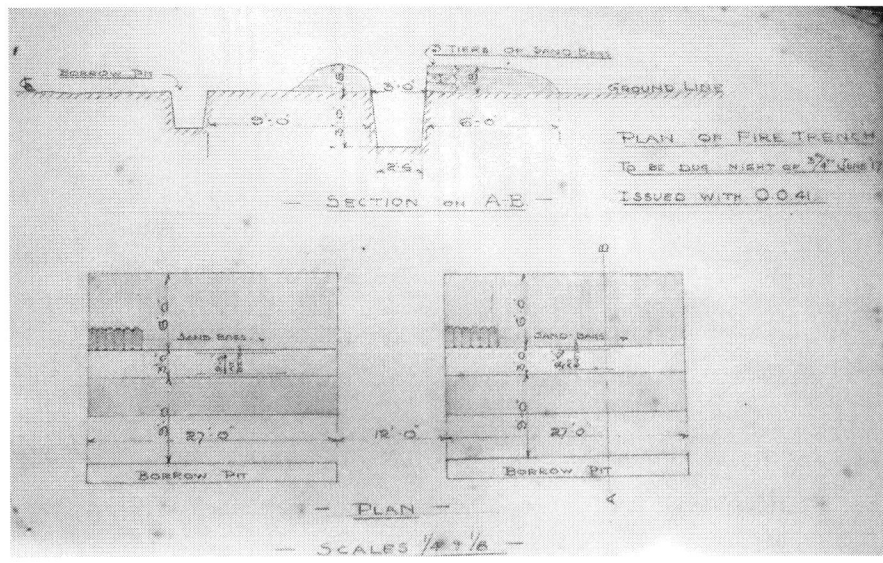

From Officer Commanding, 11th S.Lancs Regt. (Pioneers).

To C.R.E., 30th Division, Headquarters G., 30th Division.

I have to submit report on work carried out during the night 3rd/4th June, 1917.

The 200th Field Coy R.E. reported at 12-40 a.m. their Wire laid out, as per C.R.E. letter No.2477 dated 1.6.17.

The 202nd Field Coy R.E. reported at 1 a.m. their Wire laid out, as per C.R.E. letter No.2477 dated 1.6.17.

11th South Lancs Regt. The Coy on the left started work about 11-10 p.m.

The Coy on the right was considerably delayed in getting out on to the work, and did not actually commence much before 12 midnight.

77 Fire Bays and 2 Strong Points were completed the trench being dug in all cases to a depth of 3ft and in some cases rather more.

Parapet and Parados completed.

As all Coys had completed the Fire Bays by about 1 a.m., and as the enemy at that time were fairly quiet, I gave orders for the Coys to start the traverses.

All Traverses were begun, and 24 finished.

Enemy Action. The enemy were shelling fairly heavily the trench dug by the Division on our Left, and which joins on to the one we dug tonight.

They either saw or suspected that we were digging a trench as the left Coys were subjected to fairly heavy machine gun fire soon after 1 a.m., all of which went high.

Enemy artillery also fired 50 or 60 H.E's and Shrapnel Shells.

Casualties on the work. One wounded.

On returning from work, the Battalion ran into a very heavy Gas Shell Barrage, which lasted the whole way back to Camp, where it was also very bad.

Small Box Respirators were at once put on, but as the shells came very suddenly and in large numbers, many of the men must have inhaled a certain amount of the Gas before they could put their Helmets on.

At present there are 2 Officers and 12 men under treatment.

The Medical Officer in charge does not consider it advisable for the men to work for 24 hours. We left the work at 2 a.m.

Lt.Colonel.

4.6.17   Comdg 11th S.Lancs Regt.(Pioneers)

OPERATION ORDER No. 42.

by

Lieut.Colonel. H.F. Fenn, D.S.O.,

Comdg. 11th (S) Bn. South Lancashire Regt. (Pioneers).

Reference ZILLEBEKE 1/10,000.   5th June, 1917.

1. ......ION.	An attack is being made by the 2nd Army on "Z" day.
	The 23rd Division (~~Left~~ Right of 30th Division) will be on the left of the main attack and will be responsible for the capture of the general line I.30.b.40.35 – I.30.b.3.0. – I.30.d.25.50 – I.30.d.40.35. I.36.b.45.70. 0 I.36.c.2.6. etc. and will form a protective flank along the high ground running from the vicinity of ARMAGH WOOD (I.30.a.).
	Throughout "Z" day the 30th Division will endeavour to find out if the enemy have retired on the Division front, and if opportunity arises to seize the high ground near J.19.
2. INTENTION.	It is intended to consolidate all ground gained.
3. DISPOSITION.	The Battalion will be ready to move at ½ hour's notice from "Zero hour, Z day"
4. DRESS.	Battle Order.
	Each man will carry 1 shovel, 10 sandbags, and every 4th man a pick.
	In addition each Company will carry:
	12 Axes. 4 Saws-Crosscut. 12 Billhooks. 4 Pairs Wirecutters.
	Lewis Gunners parade with their Coys, without Lewis Guns.
5. BATTN. HDQRS.	Battn Headquarters, Medical Officer, and H.Qrs. stretcher bearers will move up in the first instance to I.24.b.15.75.
	Coys will move off by Platoons at 50 yds interval.

6. DETAILS.   The following men will be left behind by each Company.

Coy. Qr.M.Sergt.   2 Cooks.   1 Shoemaker.
1 Toolman.   1 Coy Clerk.   2 Sanitary men.
1 Officers Servant.   Plus Battn Guard (if any).

H F Fenn
Lieut.Colonel.
5th June, 1917.   Comdg.11th S.Lancs Regt.(Pioneers).

OPERATION ORDER No. 42

By Major C. C. Champion, Commanding,

11th (S) Bn. South Lancashire Reg. (Pioneers).

1. The 30th Division will assault the enemy's position on our front on "Z" day, which will be notified later. The 8th Division will be on our Left, and the 24th Division on our Right.

2. The Battalion will work in parties as follows:-

    (a) Three Platoons 'D' Coy, will work on STRONG POINTS under Major E. W. NAPIER-CLAVERING, D.S.O., R.E., 200th Field Coy R.E., Each Strong Point will be for a garrison of 2 Platoons and they will be situated at:
J.15.a.40.18, J.18.c.40.65, J.21.a.06.96.

    The Commanders of these Platoons will acquaint themselves with the ground by means of the KOLRL TRENCHES at J.22.b.6.4.

    (b) 1 Platoon 'D' Coy, will maintain the Artillery Track from ZILLEBEKE past YEOMANRY POST to about I.24.a.8.8 and back to ZILLEBEKE.
This Platoon will leave ASSEMBLY AREA (present billets) at ZERO minus 3 hours, and will move to site of work by Track No. 1.

    (c) 'B' Company will prepare a Track for Artillery from OBSERVATORY RIDGE ROAD at J.24.d.4.3. to J.18.b.1.5.
A reconnoitring party will start out an hour before the Company to find the best way. It is believed that "No man's Land" about J.19.a. is water logged. The track should be kept below the sky line.

    This Company will leave ASSEMBLY AREA (Present billets) at ZERO plus 1 HOUR and will move forward to site of work by TRACK No. 1.

    (d) 2nd Lieut. H.W.Gorman and 2nd Lieut. J.E.Mercer, along with Pte Longworth W. 'B' Coy, Pte Thompson J. 'B' Coy, Pte Henderson J. 'C' Coy, Pte Finney E 'D' Coy, Pte Martin J 'D' Coy and Pte Johnson F 'D' Coy, will signpost the German trenches under Lieut. McCallum R.N.

This party, along with Lieut. McCallum R.E. will assemble at Battn. Hd.Qrs in present area at ZERO plus 1 hour and move forward by Track No. 1 to the site of the work.

(e) 'A' Company will work on Light Railways under the orders of A.D.L.R. Fifth Army.

(f) 'C' Company will be in Divisional Reserve.

(g) 1 Platoon of Infantry under 2nd Lieut. WEATHERLEY will keep in repair road from SHRAPNEL CORNER to ZILLEBEKE inclusive.
This party will leave ASSEMBLY AREA, (Present Area) at ZERO plus 3 hours.

3. Picks and shovels will be carried by parties (a) (b) (c) (f) (g) in the proportion of 1 pick to 4 shovels. Party (c) will carry a proportion of wire cutters & MAULS in addition.
All parties will carry 5 sandbags per man.

Party (a) will also carry 2 Mills Grenades per man.

4. DRESS. Battle Order. Officers will wear Privates tunics with pieces of red ribbon placed on shoulder strap as per previous orders sent to O.C. Coys.

5. Companies will turn out for work at Full Strength, only the following will be left behind.
(a) G.Q.M.S., (b) Assistant to G.Q.M.S., (c) 1 Shoemaker per Company

(d) 3 Cooks per Company. (e) Those mentioned in letter No. O.P. 100/3 dated 22nd instant.

6. O.C.s parties not working under the R.E.s will report progress every 2 hours. In the case of party (c) a report will be sent in every 2 hours, and in addition a report will be sent as soon as the Track is opened for Artillery.
All messages must be timed.

7. Messages will be sent by the Relay system of Runners, Advcd B.H.Q. (Runners Post) will be established at I.23.b.2.4.
A relay post will be established in Railway Dugouts, in Sap near by the late Battn. Headquarters, and near the Report Centre of a Brigade.

Messages may be handed in at these posts.

8. R.E. Stores, including Pickets, may be obtained at Advanced Dump at I.24.a.8.3a. (BORDER LANE DUMP) and at VALLEY COTTAGES I.23.d.1.6. Details as to these dumps and what may be obtained from them sent out to Coys under this Office No. 119/12.

9. Advanced Dressing Stations will be situated at I.24.d.6.7. I.24.a.7.4., I.24.a.2.4., I.24.c.3.9., I.23.a.6.6. DORNY I.23.c.9.6. (VALLEY COTTAGE). Advanced Dressing Station also at WOODCOTE HOUSE. I.30.a.4.2. Details re these Advanced Dressing Stations also issued in letter No. O.P. 119/12.

    Water Points in the forward area are situated at ZILLEBEKE LAKE MAPLE COPSE and wells at CRAB CRAWL Dugouts. Full details issued under this Office No. O.P.119/11.

    Ammunition Dumps and Bomb Stores are at I.24.d.10.31., I.24.d.40.78., I.24.b.23.60., I.24.b.15.60., I.24.b.40.56., I.24.a.25.40. and at I.23.b.9.8. Divisional Reserve Ammunition Dump is at BEDFORD HOUSE. Main Divisional Bomb Store at H.25.b.7.6.

10. Casualties will be reported to Bn.Hd.Qrs. not later than 2 p.m. each day, made up to and including 12 noon each day. Return 12 noon to 12 noon. Estimated casualties over 50 will be rendered at once to B.H.Q.

11. The following Officers will not go in to Action, but ..... to Advcd Corps Reinforcement Camp at a time to be notified later.

> Major G F Beal. 2nd in Command.
> Captain G J. Dixon. M.C. O.C. 'C' Coy.
> Captain H.A.Hodges. O.C. 'D' Coy.
> 2nd Lt. W Ridsdale Lewis Gun Officer.

> C.C. Champion, Major
> Commdg. 11th S Lancs Regt (Pioneers)

SECRET   No. O.P.119/12.

11th (S) Bn. S. Lancashire Regt. (Pioneers).

POSITIONS AND LOCATIONS OF R.E. DUMPS.
AMMUNITION DUMPS. MEDICAL DRESSING STATTIONS
AND AID POSTS DURING OPERATIONS.

1. Ammunition
Dumps

Ammunition Dumps are situated at:-
Right Brigade. I.24.d.10.31., I.24.d.40.76.
Battalion dumps. I.24.b.23.60.

Left Brigade. I.24.b.15.80., I.24.b.40.56.
Battalion dumps.

The Right Brigade Dump at I.24.a.25.40.

The Left Brigade Dump at I.23.5.9.8.

The Divisional Reserve Ammunition Dump is situated at
BEDFORD HOUSE.

Main Divisional Bomb Store at H.26.b.7.6.

The following may be drawn from any of the Battn. Brigade,
& Divisional Dumps:-

S.A.A. Mills Hand grenades. No.24 Rifle Grenades. Mills Rifle
Grenades. Stokes Bombs. Green Cartridges for Stokes
Bombs. Rings. Flares. V.P.A. 1" D.I. V.P.A. 1" Red (or S.O.S.
colour). V.P.A. 1½" D.I. V.P.A. 1½" Red (or S.O.S. colour).
Pistol Ammunition. Petrol Tins. (from Battn & Bis Dumps
only)

2. R.E. DUMPS.

The main 30th Division R.E. Park will be at H.27.d.0.4.
The advanced Divisions Dump is located at KRUISTRAAT
at H.18.d.4.2.

The main BATTLE DUMP (BORDER LANE DUMP) will
be located at I.24.a.8.3. This dump will be connected to a
Pack Transport Track, that will be opened shortly after Sere,
which will run to CLAPHAM JUNCTION and then on to
FITZCLARENCE FARM. Stores this Dump will contain are
shown on attached Table A. A Small Battle DUMP, Stores as
on attached Table B will be located at VALLEY
COTTAGES, I.23.d.1.6. This dump will be on the track
which will be opened as soon after Zero as possible through
I.24.d.2.2., I.19.a.4.3., I.13.d.0.4. to CLAPHAM JUNCTION.

Any of these dumps will issue on demand to any Battalion or Battery immediately after Zero.

There will be a small supply of timber, explosives &c. at the BORDER LANE DUMP for use by the TECHNICAL TROOPS only.

It is hoped that a Stone Dump will be opened about I.21.a. on Z Day.

3.MEDICAL DRESSING STATIONS &C.

Regimental Aid Posts will be established at:-
I.24.d.6.7., I.24.a.7.4., I.24.a.2.4., I.24.c.3.9.
During the earlier part of the action wounded will be cleared to these by regimental stretcher bearers.

From the Regimental Aid Posts etc wounded will be cleared by hand and down the Tramway by R.A.M.C. bearers to Collecting Stations at I.23.a.6.6. DORMY. I.23.c.9.6. VALLEY COTTAGE.

The Advanced Dressing Station will be at WOODCOTE HOUSE, I.20.c.4.2.

The various routes will be "flagged" for Walking Wounded to collect them at WHITHUIS I.19.d.0.2. from which place they will be conveyed in busses and lorries to the Corps Main Dressing Station (Lightly Wounded) 25th Field Ambulance at H.27.c.1.9.

Walking Wounded of the 8th Division will be collected at KRUISSTRAAT (H.18.d.6.5.) where such men of the 30th Division as go down that way will be attended to.

A B Diplock
Lieut & Adjt.
11th S.Lancs Regt.(Pioneers).

TABLE A.
BORDER LANE BATTLE DUMP

Sandbags.	50,000.
Barbed wire, rolls.	400.
Plain wire, rolls.	10.
French wire, coils.	250.
Screw Pickets, Long.	750.
Screw Pickets, Short.	1500.
Picks.	500.
Shovels.	1500.

TABLE B.

Sandbags.	25,000.
Barbed wire, rolls.	200.
Plain wire, rolls.	5.
French wire, coils.	120.
Screw Pickets, Long.	380.
Screw Pickets, Short.	750.
Picks.	100.
Shovels.	500.

From Officer Commanding, 11th S.Lancs Regt.

To Headquarters, 30th Division "G".

C.R.E. 30th Division.

The following is Works Report on Fire Trench dug completed and 2 Communication Trenches dug night 5/6th June, 1917.

FIRE TRENCH.   New Fire Trench is now complete.

On the left 2 forward traverses were dug as 2 of the previous ones were on very bad ground.

Total depth of trench and parapet in all traverses is 4' 5" and in some cases 5' and over.

3 Bays near I.18.d.45.60 are flooded to a depth of 2' 6".

Several other bays have an inch or two of water in the bottom.

No 2 Post at I.18.d.45.10 has about 3ft of water in it.

COMMUNICATION TRENCH.   320 yds long, running from I.18.c.4.7 to New Fire Trench at I.18.c.90.95. Average depth of wall from I.18.c.4.7 to I.18.c.75.90 is 4ft. In this part the ground is very marshy and the trench had for the most part to be built up. From I.18.c.75.90 to the new Fire trench average depth of wall 5ft, with 6ft of cover on the North side for about 75 yards.

It would be possible for men to get along this trench by day if they stooped.

Communication Trench 125 yards long running from I.18.d.3.1. to new Fire trench at I.18.d.45.25. Average depth of wall 6 ft. In the centre for a length of 10 yds the wall if 3' 6" high where trench crosses the stream.

There are 2 trees crossing trench 2' 6" from ground which require cutting through. It is possible to use this trench in daytime.

ENEMY ACTION.   Enemy were quiet, and there were no casualties.

When the Coys were returning to Billets the enemy were shelling the MENIN Road and the ECOLE with a large number of H.E. and Gas Shells.

Lieut.Colonel.

Comdg.11th S.Lancs Regt. (Pioneers).

6th June, 1917.

Place	Date	Hour	Summary of Events and Information
	03/06		[k.i.a. Pte. 20521 Bernard Davies]
	04/06		[d.o.w. Pte. 26004 William Noonan]
	07/06		[d.o.w. Pte. 20855 James Lloyd]
	08/06		[k.i.a. Pte. 20217 Thomas Hankinson]
	10/06		[k.i.a. Sjt. 20566 John Parker]
	11/06		[k.i.a. 2/Lt. Eric Champion]
	12/06		[d.o.w. Pte. 21836 William Burgess; k.i.a. Pte. 22347 Norman Leah, Pte. 21213 Samuel Watkinson, Pte. 21741 Benjamin Willett]
	14/06		[d.o.w. Pte. 21404 George Gallagher; k.i.a. Pte. 21252 Samuel Woods]
	18/06		[k.i.a. Pte. 16180 Henry Garratt]
	20/06		[d.o.w. Pte. 21452 James Cooney]
	23/06		[d.o.w. L/Cpl. 20709 Thomas Lethbridge; k.i.a. Pte. 29951 Edwin Davis]
	24/06		[d.o.w. Pte. 21318 Joseph Almond, Pte. 22189 Charles Kemp; k.i.a. Pte. 21956 Henry Byron]
	25/06		[d.o.w. Pte. 21907 William Brady; k.i.a. Cpl. 20640 John Shaw]
	26/06		[d.o.w. Pte. Pte. 21625 Martin Byrne, Pte. 22389 Terence Pierce, 2/Lt. Richard Shaw; k.i.a. L/Cpl. 22279 James Heyes, Pte. 20539 John Price]
	28/06		[k.i.a. Pte. 296824 John Barlow, Pte. 21173 William Foster, Pte. 15381 George Hill]
	29/06		[d.o.w. Pte. 20883 James McLoughlin; k.i.a. Pte. 21170 Charles Borrows]
	30/06		[k.i.a. Pte. 20993 Robert Makin]
	01/07		At the beginning of the month the Battalion occupied dugouts and shelters in the CHAU SEGAR Area. Practically all the work done was in preparation for the Operations which were to open at the end of the month. It consisted

Place	Date	Hour	Summary of Events and Information
			of the construction and upkeep of forward trenches, the making and maintainance of tracks, and the repair of roads damaged by Shell fire. Communication trenches were constructed between RITZ STREET and WELLINGTON CRESCENT - passing through Assembly Trenches built the previous month by the Battalion - and between VINCE ST. & GOUROCK STREET. The activity of the enemy made maintenance parties upon VINCE ST. ZILLEBEKE ST and the Trenches North and South of ZILLEBEKE LAKE a constant necessity.
			Roads which also required continual attention were the OBSERVATORY RIDGE ROAD & the SHRAPNEL CORNER - ZILLEBEKE ROAD.
	02/07		[k.i.a. Sjt. 20736 Edward Pickles]
	05/07		[d.o.w. Pte. 20091 William Forshaw, Cpl. 20041 Francis Sutton]

11th (S) Bn. South Lancashire Regiment. (Pioneers).

WORKS REPORT FOR THE WEEK ENDING JULY 4TH. 1917.

TRENCHES. LENGTH DUG. DEPTH &c.

A Coy ZILLEBEKE ST & VINCE ST. 310 yds Trench cleaned.
1platn. 260 " " Boards repaired &
relaid.
15 " " Revetted.
100 " " Drained.

B Coy COMMUNICATIONS TRENCH between a point 200 yds W of
Junction of VINCE ST & BORDER LANE & JUNCTION OF
LOVERS WALK & GOUROCK ST.
200 yds Trench Excavated, depth 5ft
& width 4ft top and 2ft
bottom.
Trench Boards laid full length.

C Coy COMMUNICATIONS TRENCH from WELLINGTON
CRESCENT TO 'D' TRENCH, thro' A B & C Trenches.
340 yds Trench (approx.) Digging is
finished. Only needs
Sandbagging & trench
boarding.
30 yds of trench boards laid down.
Average depth trench 5' 6"

D Coy FENN LANE (A Trench) Finishing off trench to average depth
of 5' 0" with additional parapet
3 sandbags high. 60 yards of
new trench dug to average
depth of 2' 6"

RIDGE ST. (B Trench) 250 yds dug to average depth of 3' 6"
with additional parapet 3
sandbags high.
50 yds parados heightened by 3 rows
of sandbags.

			Trench boards laid over approx. 105 yards.
Cpy. 8th	NEW C.T. DUG from RITZ ST to WELLINGTON CRESCENT (nr. R.Sussex Regt. YEOMANRY POST) via A.B.C & D Trenches.		
		430	ydsTrench dug. Average depth 4' 6"
	'C' TRENCH.	300	yds (approx.) Dug (excluding Traverses) average depth 4' 6"
1 Sect. 'B' Coy. 2 TEST STATIONS.		7	feet square completed.
2 Platns 'A' Coy ROADS.		138	Shell holes filled. 5 craters filled. Roads made passable for traffic & kept in repair.
1 Pn of 'A' Coy. SCREENS.		490	yds repaired, replaced and erected.

Major.

5.7.17   Comdg.11th S.Lancs Regt. (Pioneers).

11th (S) Bn. South Lancashire Regiment. (Pioneers).

ZILLEBEKE ST. Four or Five Trench Boards are missing. When these are replaced, a maintenance party of 10 or 12 men required as the enemy is continually blowing in trench.

VINCE STREET. Maintenance party required.

'A' TRENCH. Length of trench approx.. 300 yards. Average depth 4' 6". Parapet sandbagged for about 45 yards. 32 Trench boards dumped in this trench but not laid.

'B' TRENCH. Approx length 750 yards. First 160 yards from VINCE ST trench-boarded and sandbagged. 75 yards average depth 4ft 6 ins and sandbagged, but no trench-boards. After this point 100 yards very shallow but sandbagged. Next 140 yards average depth 4ft and sandbagged. Next 180 yards average depth 6ft but very wet. From here northwards the Canadian Tunnellers are working. These measurements are round the traverses not straight across.

SOUTH COMMUNICATION TRENCH from WELLINGTON CRESCENT to RITZ ST.

Full depth from Wellington Crescent to 'B' Trench and trenchboarded, except last 15 yards into 'B' Trench where there is much water. From 'B' to 'C' Trench length 60 yards, average depth 3ft. From 'C' to 'D' Trench length about 70 yards, average depth 4ft 6 inches ready to be trench-boarded.

NORTH COMMUNICATION TRENCH was dug by one of your Coys.

430 yards trench dug, average depth 4' 6".

'C' TRENCH. 300 yards (approx.) Dug average depth 4' 6". Dug by one of your Coys.

To O.C. 8th Royal Sussex Regt.(Pioneers).

The above is a rough report on the condition of the Trenches in the Forward Area as left by this Battalion.

Major

6.7.17   Comdg.11th S.Lancs Regt. (Pioneers).

Place	Date	Hour	Summary of Events and Information
	07/07		On the night of 6th/7th, the 30th Division was relieved by the 18th Division, Headquarters moving back to NORDAUQUES on the 7th. The Field Companies remained in the forward area, being employed as follows:
			200th Field Coy. R.E. working under the orders of C.R.E. 18th Division.
			201st Field Coy. R.E. working under the orders of C.E. II Corps.
			202nd Field Coy. R.E. working under the orders of C.R.E. 8th Division.
			One Company, 11th South Lancs (Pioneers) working under C.R.E. 18th Division.
			Three Coys, 11th South Lancs (Pioneers) working under C.R.E. 8th Division. [30th Division C.R.E. War Diary]
	07/07		Sentence of Dismissal by General Court Martial in case of T/Lieut. J.G.CULSHAW, 11th Bn. South Lancashire Regt., commuted to Severe Reprimand by Field Marshal Commanding in Chief. [25th Division A&Q War Diary]

2nd Lieut. W. Ridsdale

I shall be glad if you will make out draft for WAR DIARY which will have to be sent in to the Division tonight. Rough details appended.

A.B. Diplock
Lt & Adjt.
8.7.17   11th S. Lancs Regt. (Pioneers).

On the 31.5.17.   Arrived at ECOLE, East of YPRES.

On the 3/4th.6.17   New Trench dug (details attached).

On the 13.6.17   Moved to Railway Embankment Dugouts.

On the 27.6.17   moved to CHAE SEGARD area.

Usual trenches dug, including the new Assembly Trenches "A" "B" "C" Trenches and one Communication Trench (Southern one). See papers attached.

Place	Date	Hour	Summary of Events and Information
	08/07		[k.i.a. Pte. 20158 Thomas Kelly]
	10/07		[d.o.w. Pte. 20055 Henry Bennett]
	13/07		On the 13th 'A' Company left the Battalion and the area, for the remainder of the month to work under the direction of the A.D.L.R. Fifth Army.
	13/07		On the 13th one Company of the 11th South Lancs were taken away, to be employed on Light Railway work under the A.D.L.R. Fifth Army..
			[30th Division C.R.E. War Diary]
	14/07		[k.i.a. Pte. 20948 John Edwards, Pte. 22391 Henry Roughsedge]
	16/07		[k.i.a. Pte. 21494 George Sanderson, Pte. 21880 James Wignall]

SECRET   No.O.P.100/4.

11th (S) Bn. S. Lancashire Regt. (Pioneers).
INSTRUCTIONS FOR OFFENSIVE OPERATIONS.

Number of O.R. to take part in Action.

Further to my O.P.100/3 dated 22nd inst., the following will also be left behind with the Company Hd.Qrs., and will not move forward without instructions.

C.Q.M.S.	1
Assistant.	1.
Cooks.	2.
Shoemakers.	1.

All other ranks employed on Coy Duties will parade with their Companies, who should be as strong as possible in all cases.

O.C. Coys will send in to Orderly Room by 8 p.m. on Y night the strength of their Parties for Work, and give details in the case of a company sending out more than 1 party on any one task. i.e. If a company has been allotted 2 or 3 different tasks for the operations, 2 or 3 different sets of figures will be required.

A B Diplock
Lieut & Adjt.
11th S.Lancs Reg. (Pioneers)

24.7.17.

Place	Date	Hour	Summary of Events and Information
	30/07		[d.o.w. Pte. 19401 James Caddick]
	31/07		Details of work &c on 31st July, 1917 on sheet attached.
			Casualties during the month. Officers. Wounded. 2nd Lieut R J Struthers, 2nd Lieut R.L. Leake; Wounded Still duty, 2nd Lieut W.J. Owen, 2nd Lieut S.T.E. Clench.
			Other Ranks. Killed 6. Wounded 76 (2 of which have since D of Wounds) Wounded, Still duty 17. The following N.C.O. and two men awarded the Military Medal for conspicuous gallantry.
			No. 20567 L/Cpl BLAKE W. 20842 Pte Orford J. No. 21825 Simpson J. No. 21420 L/Cpl Saxon M. 21965 Pte Robinson J V.
			C C Champion Lt. Colonel. Comdg. 11th S. Lancs Regt. (Pioneers).
			[d.o.w. Pte. 20828 Albert Hall; k.i.a. Pte. 39481 John Coombes, Pte. 203184 John Corbett, L/Cpl. 21086 Thomas Dillon]

From Adjutant.

To O.C. 'A' Coy.

Following Copy forwarded:-

"Fifth Army wire begins aaa Situation up to about 10 am 14th Corps captured GREEN LINE to time and were in touch on both flanks aaa They have since captured passages of STEEBECK except on Left Flank where situation unclear aaa A Counter attack against the junction of the Two Armies was reported by the First French Army to have been repulsed aaa F.O.O. reports 3rd Guard Fusiliers BERLIN COCKCHAFERS smashed by them aaa Opposition on this Corps front does not appear to have been severe aaa 18th Corps reports left div. on GREEN LINE with post across STEEBECK and bridgehead at M---- BERATSA and in touch with right div. which has also reached the stream ... This Div. reported to have taken ST JULIEN aaa 19th Corps left Div. established advanced post BORDER HOUSE and POND FARM rest of Div and whole of Right Div on BLACK LINE Right Div. met with considerable opposition about SQUARE FARM FREZENBERG and STATION BUILDINGS aaa 2nd Corps situation still obscure on centre and right aaa Left Div gained BLACK LINE and commenced to advance to GREEN LINE on time aaa Centre Div was held up in front of GLENCORSE WOOD and INVERNESS COPSE where heavy fighting has been going on aaa Left and right of right Div believed to have reached BLACK LINE but centre held up by post about J.25.central aaa Considerable enemy movement in front of 2nd Corps and several counter attacks reported unconfirmed forward movement field artillery being successfully carried out on 14th 19th 18th Corps fronts aaa Tanks everywhere reported moving forward aaa Enemy reported heavily shelling J.7 from S.E. and enfilading BLACK LINE W. of POMMERN REDOUBT from direction of BRODSEINDE Cross roads rough estimate of prisoners to date 1750 have reached Corps cages aaa ends aaa

A. B. DIPLOCK, Lieut. & Adjt.

To O.C. 'A' Coy.

Following is copy of wire received from Division for your information.

Fifth Army Wire timed 10 p.m. 31/7/17 begins aaa Situation 14th Corps line runs U.20.d.0.6. PENSON FARM RUISPAU FARM U.27.cent. with Posts E of STEENBECK U.27.cent AU BON GITE REGINA CROSS counter attacks on AU BON GITE dispersed by Arty M.G. and rifle fire with heavy casualties to enemy aaa 18th Corps U.28.b.3.3. FERDINAND FARM REGINA CROSS to STEENBECK West of ST JULIEN with posts at U.26.d.4.2. and D.91 aaa 19th Corps BORDER HOUSE POMMERN CASTLE DEENA FARM VAMPIRE POTSDAM aaa Heavy counterattack on POMMERN CASTLE from HILL 33 in progress 2nd Corps D.26.d.2.2 WESTHOEK CROSS ROADS J.7.d.6.7. J.14.c.2.5. J.19.b.5.2. J.23.a.3.4. J.31.a.8.8. aaa 1st French Army lines runs T.11.c.8.1. T.11.d.8.4. BIXSCHOOTS GUIRASSIER FARM SCOTTISH HOUSE REDMILL NORTEKEEG CABRET U.20.b.4.7. aaa Second Army captured HOLLEBEKE VILLAGE and LA BASSE VILLAGE and report capture 6 Officers 340 O.R. aaa Fifth Army captured 71 Officers 3060 O.R. aaa 4 field guns and 1 How, brought in.

30th Division 2 p.m.

1.8.1917.

A B Diplock Lt & Adjt.,
11th S.Lancs Reg. (Pioneers).

WORK OF THE BATTALION on ZERO DAY (31st July, 1917)

The Work on ZERO DAY allotted to the Battalion - less the 1 Company employed under the A.D.L.R. - consisted of opening up tracks to captured territory for the passage of guns and transport and of constructing strong points, in conjunction with the R.E.s, a short distance behind the new British Front Lines.

Under ordinary weather conditions the actual task of making fresh tracks and maintaining the old ones would have produced no unsurmountable difficulties. To lay out "Fine Weather Tracks" in torrential rain proved to be quite another proposition. Very quickly the tracks became little more than quagmires, and work upon them had to be confined to pegging them out, clearing them of barbed wire and other obstacles and filling in or bridging old trenches. A shortage of hard material for filling in the shell holes & trenches added to the difficulties. Furthermore the parties working were shelled persistently.

'B' Company were engaged on the Artillery Track from OBSERVATORY RIDGE ROAD to STILING CASTLE. They left Chau Segard Area 1 hour after Zero. Everything was done to drain the track and to find wood etc. with which to fill in holes, but along it mud was over the boot tops However by 7 p.m. the way was open for Light Guns as far as the old German Front Line. Owing to the activity of the enemy's Machine guns and snipers, attempts in daylight to work beyond the ridge which was continuously shelled - had to be abandoned.

In the evening 'C' Coy which had been in Divisional Reserve continued work on the Track. Order were received to carry it as far forward as possible as a Track for Mules and to divert it under the ridge out of view in order to escape the heavy shelling. This was done. 'B' Coy spent the night in trenches near the Work, and, with the assistance of 'C' Coy carried on with the track during the day. Both Coys returned to Camp the following evening.

Casualties were 1 Officer wounded, Other Ranks killed one, Wounded 30.

1 Platoon of 'D' Coy which set out before Zero, from Chau Segard was engaged on an Artillery Track from ZILLBEKE to I.24.a.8.8. and back. Similar difficulties to those upon the track mentioned above were encountered, but this track was successfully opened and maintained and was early in use by the Artillery.

Casualties. Other Ranks Killed one, Wounded nine.

3 Platoons of 'D' Coy were engaged with part of 200th Field Coy R.E. in constructing Strong Points. This party remained "Standing to" in Zillebeke Street from 7.30 a.m. to 8 p.m. during which time there was very heavy shelling. At 8 p.m. instructions were received to proceed forward and to make 3 strong points

just behind the "Blue Line". These were successfully completed, in face of exceptionally adverse conditions.

Casualties. Other Ranks Wounded 18, Wounded & Returned to duty 2.

Since the particular tasks allotted to the Battalion for ZERO day and Zero day plus one, work has consisted of the maintenance of these Tracks and Tracks Nos. 10 and 11 in addition. The only exception was on the night of August 2nd when 50 men worked with 200th Field Coy R.E. on wiring the new British front Line for a distance of 900 yards.

Upon Zero day and upon August 2nd, South Lancs Transport provided men and Pack animals for conveying R.E. Material to the line. Several animals were killed. On Zero day, one pack mule lead was wounded; on August 2nd one was killed and two wounded.

C C Champion   Lt. Colonel.
Comdg. 11th S. Lancs Regt. (Pioneers).
9th August 1917.

WORK CARRIED OUT BY THE TECHNICAL TROOPS 30TH DIVISION DURING ACTIVE OPERATIONS FROM 31-7-17 TO 3-8-17

11th South Lancs (Pioneers)

One Company of the 11th South Lancs was taken away for work on Light Railways under the A.D.L.R. Fifth Army, thus only leaving 3 Coys. for Divisional work. In addition to the work already given above, this Battalion did exceptional good work on upkeep of old, and construction of new roads.

A road for Artillery from ZILLEBEKE to just West of SANCTUARY WOOD (I.24.a.8.7.) was opened out and used by our Artillery a few hours after Zero, one platoon was employed on this work and on keeping this road in repair.

The OBSERVATORY RIDGE ROAD was opened for traffic from RODKIN HOUSE to our old front line about J.19.d.8.3. by night of 31st and to German front line about J.19.c.1.4. by the morning of 1st August, and from there a mile track was on another 500 yards in the direction of STIRLING CASTLE by morning of 3rd August. Work was very much delayed owing to very bad weather and to heavy shelling and M.G. fire which caused considerable casualties.

They also kept in repair the main road from SHRAPNEL CORNER to ZILLEBEKE and Tracks 10 and 11, work again being much delayed by bad weather, which turned all tracks into deep mud.

[30th Division C.R.E. War Diary]

Place	Date	Hour	Summary of Events and Information
In the Field	01/08 to 31/08		At the beginning of the month the Battn was still in the CHATEAU SEGARD Area, S of YPRES.
			Work was done upon forward Tracks and between the 1st & the 6th when the Battn. left the area, casualties were 1 O.R. Killed and 15 O.R. wounded.
			Upon the 5th the Battn marched to RENINGHELST Stn and entrained for BOIEWAERSENIE.
			Here it stayed until the 7th, when it marched to STRAZEELE & remained under canvas in the training area until the 11th inst. On that date the Battn marched to EPSOM CAMP, Nr Westoutre and began training.
			On the 16th however the Battn moved by road to VIERSTRAAT where work was begun upon the MESSINES RIDGE DEFENCES.
			Upon the 22nd inst. the Battalion moved from VIERSTRAAT to SPY FARM, Nr. LINIENHOEK taking over its present quarters from the Pioneers of the 4th Australian Divn.
			Work was done upon MANCHESTER ST (Forward C.T.), forward roads and camouflage.
			The casualties between the 8th and the end of the month were two O.R.s wounded, making a total 1 O.R. killed and 17 O.R.s wounded during the month.
			C C Champion Lt. Colonel. Comdg. 11th S. Lancs Regt. (Pioneers).
	03/08		[d.o.w. Pte. 21755 James Heslip]

Place	Date	Hour	Summary of Events and Information

STATEMENT OF CASUALTIES 24th July to 4th Aug. 1917

		Killed	Wounded	Missing	Total
11th South Lancs. Regt.	Officers	-	2	-	2
	O.R.	3	70	-	73
	Total	3	72	-	75

[30th Division A&Q War Diary]

05/08   [d. Pte. 21964 Robert Birkett]

08/08   [d.o.w. Pte. 20650 Robert Robinson]

11/08   [d.o.w. Pte. 36522 William Smith]

16/08   On the 16th the Divisional Engineers and 11th Bn. South Lancs Regt. (Pioneers) marched to the VIERSTRAAT Area being placed at the disposal of C.E. IX Corps from the 17th for work on the Ridge Defences. Each Brigade attached 100 infantry to their affiliated Field Company as a working party for this work, and this arrangement was subsequently made permanent. [30th Division C.R.E. War Diary]

23/08   On the 23rd the 30th Division took over the line from the 4th Australian Division, Field Companies moving to the new area on the 22nd, and Headquarters R.E. moving to DRANOUTRE on the 23rd.

Field Companies were employed as follows:
200th Field Coy. R.E. - on BOB STREET & DORSET STREET Communication Trenches under orders of C.R.E.

201st Field Coy. R.E. - "Y" line under orders of C.R.E.

202nd Field Coy. R.E. - Front line under orders of G.O.C. 21st Infantry Brigade.

11th South Lancs Rgt. - MANCHESTER STREET Communication Trench, Roads and Screens.
[30th Division C.R.E. War Diary]

Place	Date	Hour	Summary of Events and Information
	01/09 to 30/09		At the beginning of the month the Battalion was still in the Camp taken over on the 22nd of August 1917 from the 4th Australian Division Pioneers. (SPY FARM Nr LINDENHOEK). Work was continued during the month upon MANCHESTER ST (Forward C.T.) forward roads, camouflage, and from the 13th, a Company & half employed on the erection of NISSEN HUTS in the vicinity of KEMMEL, also from the 17th inst 1 Platoon engaged in the preparation of Winter Quarters for a portion of the Battalion. During the month the total casualties were 10 Other Ranks wounded, 1 of whom Died.
			C C Champion Lt. Colonel. Comdg. 11th S. Lancs Regt. (Pioneers).
	07/09		[d. Sjt. 20378 Job Wilson]
	09/09		[d.o.w. Pte. 21815 John Ackers]
Spy Farm Nr Kemmel	01/10 to 31/10		The Battalion was still at SPY FARM, the camp taken over on the 22nd August, 1917 from the 4th Australian Divisional Pioneers.
			Work was continued on Manchester St (Forward C.T.) until the 30th/31st Octr., on which date the trench was finished. Work was commenced the following night on DORSET ST. and BOB ST. Communication Trenches.
			During the month work was also carried out on the Roads in the Divisional Area, by 1 Company on NISSEN HUTMENTS in the vicinity of KEMMEL, and 1 Company on the preparation of WINTER QUARTERS at N.24.c.4.5., and work on SCREENS in Div. Area. Half Company also employed on the construction and laying of a Tramline in the forward area, running from In. De Sterke Cabaret O.15.a.3.2., to RAVINE O.10.d.10.70.
			On the night 26/27th Octr. 1917, 2nd Lieut. J.

Place	Date	Hour	Summary of Events and Information

Holmes, and 5 Other Ranks went out on Patrol from Post No.13 at O.17.central for the purpose of reconnoitering an enemy Post at BANG FARM and vicinity. Patrol left Post.13 at 12-30 a.m. and continued a parallel route to VERNE Road until they reached the German Wire, which runs N & S and parallel to the Low Fm - Bang Fm Road and about 20 yards on the West side of the road. Wire only a few strands on Screw Pickets and easily passable No actual gaps however were found in the wire. The ground west of Bang Fm. was found to be in good condition. When patrol approached enemy wire 6 Germans were observed carrying material which they dumped at O.17.b.90.25 and 25 yards from patrol. They commenced to dig in very muddy ground near the hedge. 2 of the enemy remained on Sentry, but as Patrol orders were to obtain information only, they remained stationary and later examined the trenches in the vicinity, of which were found to have fallen in, and apparently disused.

On the night of the 27/28th Oct. 1917, Lieut W.J. Owen and 5 Other Ranks went out on Patrol from Post No.13 for the purpose of reconnoitering the Post mentioned above, but on this occasion patrol only reached a point near VERNE Road at O.17.b.35.10 where an enemy working party was observed 30 yards ahead. At O.17.c.45.10 across the VERNE Road is a double belt of concertina barbed wire, each belt 3 yards apart and each 50 ft in length and which appears to be a road barricade only.

On the 28th/29th Octr. 1917 a Patrol consisting of 2nd Lieut, J. Holmes, 1 Warrant Officer and 9 Other Ranks, went out from No.13 Post at O.17.central at 11-45 p.m. for the purpose of continuing reconnaisance of BANG FARM, and if possible to secure a prisoner. When Patrol had proceeded yards past our own wire, an enemy

Place	Date	Hour	Summary of Events and Information

party of 15 to 20 strong was observed walking to and fro' from O.17.b.63.15 on the VERNE ROAD to the opposite hedge at O.17.b.60.32. The Patrol Leader and N.C.O. advanced to within close view of this party, at the same time protecting their flanks with the remainder of the patrol. As the enemy party considerably outnumbered our Patrol, nothing could be done at the moment other than wait developments. From the noise of the Iron Pickets being used and pairs of the enemy halting at each Picket, it was obvious that the enemy was wiring. They continued this work for an hour and a quarter. The enemy party was protected by 3 groups of double sentries behind trees on the VERNE Road, each group being 20 yards apart and held connection by occasional patrols between each group.

During the month one man was slightly wounded by an aeroplane dud shell, but remained at duty.

H F Fenn   Lt. Colonel.
Comdg. 11th S. Lancs Regt. (Pioneers).

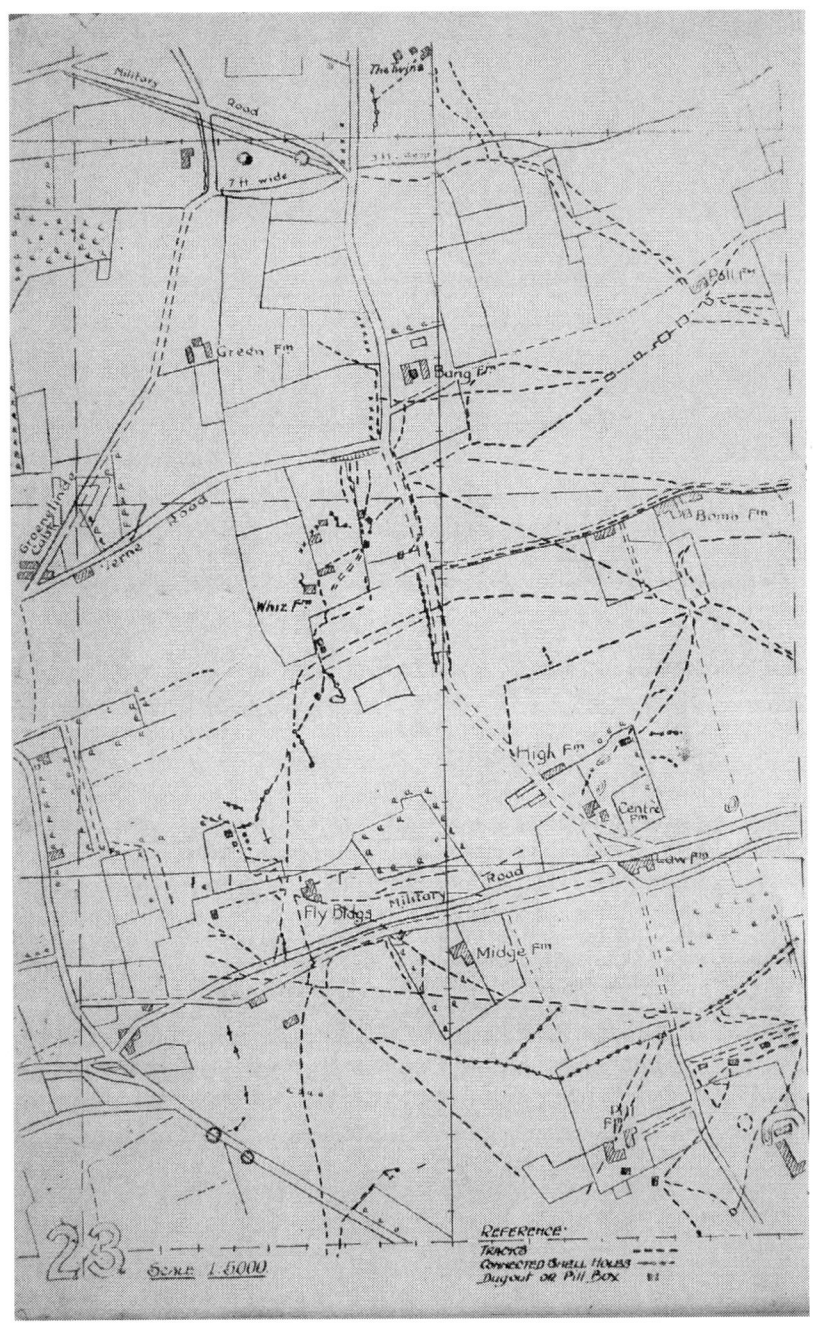

Bang Farm

SECRET   No.O.P.1306/12.

11th (S) Bn. S. Lancashire Regt. (Pioneers).

DEFENCE SCHEME.

1. ACTION IN CASE OF ATTACK.

In case of a hostile attack, the 11th S. Lancs Regt. will come under the orders of the G.O.C. Right Brigade.

The Battalion less 4 Lewis Guns at Wytschaete, will move up to LINEN FARM via Track 'C' or South of it.

2. DISTRIBUTION OF BATTALION.

Battalion Headquarters. 'C' Coy and ½ B Coy in LINEN FM.

'A' Coy and ½ B Coy in Trench S.E. of the Farm.

'D' Coy will be in Trench N.E. of the Farm.

3. RIGHT BRIGADE HEADQUARTERS.

Brigade Headquarters will move forward to TORRENS FARM.

4. RECONNAISANCE OFGROUND.

As the Battalion would probably be used for Counter Attack, all officers and as many N.C.O.s as possible must be acquainted with the ground lying East of LINEN FARM and should also be acquainted with Track 'C' which commences just South of Brigade Headquarters, Regent Dugouts, and travels round L'Eafer Wood.

5. AMMUNITION ..... &C.

Arrangements will be made to carry any Lewis Gun Ammunition by hand.

Each Company will draw 5 boxes of Detonated Bombs from the Battalion Guard Room, near Battalion Hd.Qrs. on receiving orders to move to Assembly Positions.

The Transport Officer will arrange to bring up a further supply of bombs, ammunitions and supply of water. The Bombing Sergeant will report to the T'port Officer and detonate all Bombs & Grenades.

Very Pistols will be taken up, and a supply of Very Lights obtained from Bde. Hd.Qrs. en route.

6. COMMUNICATIONS.

There is a Visual Station (Divisional) on KEMMEL HILL immediately below the Tower. This station is in visual communication with LUMM FARM.

Each Company will detail 2 Orderlies to report to Bn. Hd.Qrs. immediately on receipt of orders to move to forward assembly Positions.

7. MOVEMENT TO ASSEMBLY POSITIONS.

On receiving the order to move to Assembly positions Coys will move to positions mentioned in para 2 independently.

Coys report their leaving to Bn. Hd.Qrs. at SPY FARM.

Coys report their arrival to Bd. Hd.Qrs. at LUMM FARM.

8. S.O.S. SIGNAL.

(1) The S.O.S. Signal will be sent up by order of any Officer.

The signal will be repeated until our artillery barrage opens fire. The message will also be sent by telephone to Brigade Headquarters in the following form:-

RIGHT (or Left) SUBSECTOR S.O.S.

(2) The following S.O.S. signals are available:-

In use (Night)   Rifle Grenade Signal – parachute – with 3 colours – red over green over yellow.

(Day)   Mortar Signal issuing red smoke.

First Change. (If necessary) Rifle Grenade Signal – parachute – light changing from white to green.

Second Change. (If necessary). 1½" Very Light – parachute- light changing from white to red.

As circumstances permit, this last will also be made into a Rifle Grenade Signal.

Albert Dean
Lt & Adjt
for Lt.Colonel
Comdg.11th S. Lancs Regt. (Pioneers)

13/10/1917

Place	Date	Hour	Summary of Events and Information
	22/10		[k.i.a. Pte. 20963 Richard Melling]
Spy Farm	01/11 to 30/11		The Battalion was still at Spy farm in the same camp as taken over from the 4th Aust. Division Pioneers on the 22nd August 1917. Work was continued on DORSET & BOB ST. Communication Trenches. NISSEN HUTS were constructed in the vicinity of KEMMEL for Brigade Reserve.

Tramway Line was laid in the forward area, running from In de Sterke Cabaret O.15.a.3.2. to the RAVINE O.10.d.10.70. All roads in the forward Divisional Area were repaired and maintained. Work done on all screens in the Divisional Area. Winter Quarters for the Battalion were continued with at N.24.c.4.5.

The foregoing work was carried on by the Battalion until the 8th Nov. 1917 when orders were received from the Division for the Battalion to be prepared to move on the following morning to BAILLEUL. On the 9th November, we were relieved by the 5th Australian Pioneer Battn. who took over SPY FARM Camp, and all work in the Divisional Area which the Battalion had been employ on. On the 11th inst Battalion moved by BUS from BAILLEUL to YPRES (S.W.)

On the 13th inst. The Battalion was ordered to move to Salvation Corner N.W. of YPRES and took over the Camp of the 2nd Bn. Canadian Pioneers. On the 14th inst the Battalion was employed on forward roads in the Passchendale Sector, in order to get these roads open for and repaired for Field Artillery &c. for a contemplated operation. On the 24th inst. Orders were received for the Battalion to move to I.31.d.5.5. (Sheet 28) Nr. VORMEZEELES, and take over the camp and work from the 13th Gloucestershire Regt. Owing to the urgency of the opening and clearing of the ST.JEAN-

Place	Date	Hour	Summary of Events and Information

BELLEVUE Road, two Coys were ordered to remain behind to complete the work, and join Battalion on 25th at I.31.d.5.5. All work was taken over from the Gloucestershire Regt. and consisted of work on PERTH AVENUE C.T., and construction and maintenance of all Plankroads Mule Tracks and Infantry Duckboard tracks.

On 26th November, orders were received to move 2 Coys to ZILLEBEKE BUND, on 29th a fourth Coy to ZILLEBEKE BUND, and on 30th remaining Coy to RAILWAY DUGOUTS. Battn Hd. Qr & details moved to ZILLEBEKE BUND on 1st December, 1917.

On and from 26th November, 1917 the Battalion work was re-arranged and more work taken on which included 1 Coy under orders of G.O.C. Brigade in Line, 1 Coy under orders of Field Coy R in Line on Supporting Points.

Casualties incurred during the month were Other Ranks Killed 1, Wounded 9, Wounded, still duty.

H F Fenn   Lt. Colonel.
Comdg. 11th S. Lancs Reg. (Pioneers).

14/11 On the 14th, Headquarters R.E., the 3 Field Coys. and 11th South Lancs Pioneers were detached from the 30th Division and were temporarily attached to the CANADIAN CORPS in the PASSCHENDAELE Sector.

When the VIII Corps took over this sector from the CANADIAN CORPS, the technical troops of the 30th Division remained at the same work, and were returned to the VIII Corps.
[30th Division C.R.E. War Diary]

17/11 Two companies of the 11th South Lancs Pioneers will take over the work of the 9th E.R.R. on the SOUTH ROAD from midnight 18th/19th and will work under the orders of the

Place	Date	Hour	Summary of Events and Information
			O.C. 202nd Field Coy. R.E.
			One company of the 11th South Lancs Pioneers will work on the NORTH ROAD under the orders of C.R.E. 14th Division.
			One company of the 11th South Lancs Pioneers will hold themselves in readiness to proceed to the STEENVOORDE Area. [30th Division C.R.E. War Diary]
	20/11		[k.i.a. Pte. 20648 Hugh Thomas]
	23/11		The 11th South Lancs Pioneers will move to the 30th Divl. area as follows:
			Headquarters and 2 companies on 24th.
			2 companies on 25th.
			They will take over work and billets from the 13th Gloucestershire Regt. (Pioneers) who will also move in two parties on 24th and 25th.
			Work will therefore not stop on the BELLEVUE Road.
			The 13th Gloucesters are located at VOORMEZEELE at E.31.d.5.5. with Transport at E.16.b.8.8.
			Advanced parties will be sent ahead to take over work and billets early tomorrow morning. A rear party of 1 officer and 10 men will remain behind to show incoming Battalion work and billets. [30th Division C.R.E. War Diary]
	30/11		After the 27th the distribution of work was as follows:
			11th Bn. South Lancs.
			1 Company working under the orders of G.O.C. Brigade in the line.
			1 Company working on the Reserve Line under the orders of O.C. 200th Field Coy. R.E.

Place	Date	Hour	Summary of Events and Information
			1 Company on Roads and Tracks.
			1 Company working on PERTH AVENUE. [30th Division C.R.E. War Diary]
Zillebeke Bund	01/12 to 31/12		Battalion Hd. Qrs. and 3 Coys still in Dugouts at ZILLEBEKE BUND. 1 Coy in Dugouts (Railway).
			Disposition the same as reported in last War Diary for November, 1917. Work carried on during the month of December as under -
			1 Company on Tracks (Infantry Duckboard Tracks). 1 Company on Mule Tracks.
			1 Company under the orders of G.O.C. Brigade in Left Sector.
			1 Company under orders of O.C. Field Coy R.E. in Line.
			2nd Lieut. Holman A.E. and 2nd Lieut. J.J. Acton wounded during December, 1917. Other Ranks - Killed 4, Wounded 20.
			Sergt. W. Smart, L/Cpl. Bishop J. & Pte Prescott W. awarded Military Medal for Gallantry in Action in the Field.
			H F Fenn Lt. Colonel. Comdg. 11th S. Lancs Regt. (Pioneers).
	02/12		[k.i.a. Pte. 20376 John Woods]
	03/12		[k.i.a. Pte. 20777 Charles Gill]
	04/12		[d.o.w. Sjt. 20882 Herbert Wilkinson]
	09/12		[k.i.a. Pte. 39433 George Harper]
	15/12		[k.i.a. Pte. 17082 George Atkin]

1918

Place	Date	Hour	Summary of Events and Information
	01/01		At the beginning of the month the Battalion occupied Dugouts at ZILLEBEKE BUND (B.H.Q. & Coys) and RAILWAY DUGOUTS (1 Coy). Regtl Transport & Q.M. details billeted at DICKEBUSCH.
	04/01 to 05/01		Regimental Transport moved from DICKEBUSCH by march route to RACQUINGHAM, arriving there in the evening of the 5th January. Battalion moved on the 5th instant to RACQUINGHAM, proceeding by rail from DICKEBUSCH.
	08/01		Battalion and Regtl Transport moved from ACQUINGHAM to AMIENS area, marching to STEEBECQUE from where the Battalion entrained. On arrival at detraining station, LONGEAU, Battalion marched to a new area and billeted as follows:- B.H.Q. BLANGY TRONVILLE CHATEAU. 2 Coys GLISSY 2 Coys BLANGY.
			Until the 12th inst. Time spent in training.
	13/01		The Battalion and Transport proceeded to PROYART by march route, a distance of 15 miles.
	14/01		The Battalion and Transport marched from PROYART to CURCHY & ETALON area, B.H.Q. an 2 Coys being billeted at CURCHY and 2 Coys at ETALON.
			On the evening of the same date orders received for 2 Coys to move to OFFOY (3 miles W of HAM.) on the following morning by march route for attachment to XVIII Corps.
			The remaining 2 Coys ('C' & 'D') billeted with B.H.Q. at CURCHY carried on with Training until the 18th inst when orders were received that

Place	**Date**	**Hour**	**Summary of Events and Information**
			Battalion, less the 2 Coys detached, would move on the following day to NESLE for work under the orders of C.R.E. 5th Army Troops.

SECRET   Copy No 1

11th (S) Bn. South Lancashire Regt.

Order No. 1   18th Jany.1918.

Reference AMIENS SHEET 1/100,000.

1.   The 11th South Lancashire Regt. (less 2 Coys) and 202nd Field Company,
     R.E. will move from present area, in accordance with the attached Table,
     on the 19th January, 1918.

     On arrival NESLE, the 11th South Lancashire Regt. (less 2 Coys) and
     202nd Field Coy. R.E. will come under the orders of C.R.E. Fifth Army
     Troops.

     202nd Field Coy R.E. will march under the orders of O.C. 11th Bn. South
     Lancashire Regt.

2.   Intervals of 200 yards between the 11th S. Lancs. Regt. And the 202nd
     Field Coy R.E. and 25 yards between every 6 Transport vehicles will be
     maintained.

3.   Completion of move will be reported to Battn. Headquarters, at NESLE.

4.   ACKNOWLEDGE.

                                                              H.F. Fenn
                                                              Lt.Colonel
18th Jan.1918.   Commanding 11th S. Lancs. Regt. (Pioneers).

Distribution.

Copy No. 1.   War Diary
        2.   O.C. 202nd Field Coy R.E.
        3.   O.C. "C" Coy.
        4.   O.C. "D" Coy.
        5.   Transport Officer
        6.   Quartermaster
        7.   Lewis Gun Officer
        8.   File.

11/SLR War Diary

Place	Date	Hour	Summary of Events and Information
	20/01		Work commenced on the renovation of Billets &c preparatory to the 5th Army Headquarters arriving in NESLE.
	22/01		1 Officer and 50 Other Ranks proceeded by Motor Lorries to BONNEUIL CHATEAU for work on HANGARS and mens huts.
	25/01		1 Officer and 6 Lewis Gun Teams with Guns proceeded to VILLERS-ST-CHRISTOPHE and HAM for Anti-Aircraft protection, in accordance with orders received direct from XVIII Corps.
	31/01		Final dispositions of Battalion on the 31st January, 1918 -
			2 Coys located near ETREILLERS & GRAND SERAUCOURT for work under XVIII Corps. 2 Coys & Bn. Hd. Qrs at NESLE under orders of C.R.E. 5th Army Troops.
			1 Officer & 50 men at BONNEUIL CHATEAU under orders of C.R.E. 5th Army Troops.
			1 Officer & 6 Lewis Gun Sections at VILLERS-ST-CHRISTOPHE and HAM for A.A. protection.
			2nd Lieut. Helman A.E. and 2nd Lieut. J.J. Acton returned from Hospital on the 21st and 24th ins having been wounded in December 1917.
			Other Ranks Wounded 2.
			Lieut. (Captain) A.G. LEAN awarded the Military Cross for Gallant Service in the Field. London Gazette 3.1.1918.
			L/Sergt. Potter J. awarded the Distinguished Conduct Medal for gallant service in the Field. London Gazette 5.1.1918.
			Total strength of Battalion on the 31.1.1918. 37 Officers and 869 Other Ranks.
			C C Champion Major for Lt. Colonel. (A.O.D.) Cmdg 11th South Lancashire Regt. (Pioneers).

Place	Date	Hour	Summary of Events and Information
	01/02		At the beginning of the month the Battalion was located as reported in the last portion of the War Diary for the month of January, 1918.
	13/02		Work carried on as usual until the 13th Feby. 1918 when orders were received that Bn. Hd. Qrs and 2 Coys would move from NESLE on the 14th Feby. 1918 to destination as under -
			Hd. Qrs. to DRURY - 'C' Coy to ROUPY - 'D' Coy to SAVY.
	17/02		In the meantime 'C' and 'D' Coys were employed on the improvement of their Billets, after which date, they were employed on work under the orders of O.C. Field Coys R.E. preparing Defence Lines.
	20/02		'A' Coy. 3 Platoons moved from ATILLY to DURY for the purpose of erecting NISSEN HUTS of the Divisional Headquarters who moved in to DURY on the 26th Feby. 1918, remaining Platoon of 'A' arrived at DURY on the 22nd inst. to assist in erection of NISSEN HUTS.
	23/02		[30th Division takes over the front line near St Quentin in the area around Manchester Redoubt.]

At that time the Forward Zone trenches were nearly complete: the Battle Zone trenches were well wired but the trenches themselves only in most cases marked out. The front was held by two brigades each on a one battalion front: the remaining two battalions per brigade were employed in digging the trenches in the Battle Zone and training. The Battle Zone was divided into three battalion sectors with a fourth battalion, giving extra depth, in the ETREVILLERS Defences.

Battalions were detailed to sectors and thus reaped the inestimable advantage of making the actual trenches in which they knew they were to fight.

Place	Date	Hour	Summary of Events and Information
			From the time when the Division took over the line, until the day of the attack, battalions were daily at work in the trenches. Training was combined with work and took the form of the attack on, and defence of, the trenches in which the troops were working. [30th Division HQ War Diary - Narrative of Operations 21st to 30th March 1918]
	23/02		The 30th Division took over the centre of the XVIII Corps front, taking over the Northern portion from the 61st Division and the Southern portion from the 36th Division. Divisional Headquarters at HAM. Each Division became responsible for the Battle Zone in its own front. 202nd Field Coy. R.E. took over the whole of the Battle Zone on the 30th Divisional Front. The other Field Coys. took over the work in the line as follows:
			200th Field Coy. R.E. - Left Brigade Subsector - located at DOUCHY.
			201st Field Coy. R.E. - Right Brigade Subsector - located at VAUX.
			Distribution: Two sections in the line; one section with the artillery; one section back areas.
			H.Q. 1 Coy. & Transport Pioneers moved to FLUQUIERES.
			Distribution: 1 Coy attached to each Field Coy. 1 Coy employed on Divisional Headquarters and hutting. [30th Division C.R.E. War Diary]
	24/02		Captain H.J.WOOLCOCK, 11th Bn. South Lancs. Regt., appointed Divisional Agricultural Officer. [30th Division A&Q War Diary]
	26/02		On this date Bn. Hd. Qrs and Transport vacated Billets at DURY and moved to FLUQUIERES in the forward area, the 3 Platoons remaining behind

Place	Date	Hour	Summary of Events and Information
			at DURY for the purpose of finishing off erection of Nissen Huts and completing Billets. 1 Platoon of 'A' Coy moved to AUBIGNY to erect NISSEN HUTS and Bunking Barns.
	28/02		One platoon moved from DURY to FLUQUIERES for the purpose of erecting NISSEN HUTS for R.A.
	01/03		At the beginning of the month the Battalion was located as reported in the last portion of the War Diary for the month of February 1918.
			Work carried on the Forward Zone, Battle Zone & redoubts and Keeps in the SAVY - ROUPY Area. (W of ST. QUENTIN).
			A further platoon moved from DURY to FLUQUIERES for the purpose of erecting HUTS at VAUX The following is the final distribution of the Battalion on the 1st March 1918.
			'A' Coy H.Q. and 1 Platoon at DURY. 1 Platoon at AUBIGNY and 2 Platoons at FLUQUIERES.
			'B' Coy located at SAVY working under orders of 200th Field Coy R.E. in Forward Zone.
			'C' Coy located at ROUPY working under orders of 202nd Field Coy R.E. in BATTLE ZONE.
			'D' Coy located at A.8.a. (Sheet 66d N.E.) under orders of 201st Field Coy R.E. working on REDOUBTS & KEEPS (Battle Zone).
			No casualties suffered during the month of February 1918.
			H F Fenn Lt. Colonel. Comdg. 11th S. Lancs Regt. (Pioneers).
	08/03 to 20/03		On the 8th March 1918 the Battalion was reorganised from 4 Coys to 3 Coys in accordance with G.H.Q. instructions, consequently dispositions of Coys were changed and read as

Place	Date	Hour	Summary of Events and Information
			under - 'A' Coy H.Q. and 1 Platoon at ROUPY. 1 Platoon at A.3.d. (Sheet 66c N.W.) 1 Platoon at DURY. 1 Platoon at AUBIGNY. 'B' Coy H.Q. and 4 Platoons remained at SAVY WOOD. 'C' Coy H.Q. and 3 Platoons remained at ROUPY. 1 Platoon at FLUQUIERES. Work was continued until the 20th inst (inclusive).
	20/03		RE and Pioneers were located in the line according to the work they were engaged on. Their order in case of attack were: if in the Forward Zone to remain and fight under the nearest unit; elsewhere withdraw to Assembly position about ETREVILLERS. Numbers and Morale. Owing to the big leave allotment, on any one day 1,700 to 1,800 men were away on leave. This number, added to the usual large numbers away on courses, seriously deplete the fighting strength of battalions, none of which were over 600 strong on the day of attack. Since leaving Flanders, early in January, the Division had been through quiet times in peaceful sectors; this added to a long spell of fine weather had raised their morale to a very high standard. All ranks had had the scheme of defence thoroughly explained to them and had great confidence in it. Battalions in the Forward Zone realised their position, but felt confident in being able to stop t enemy. All were eager for the enemy to attack. [30th Division HQ War Diary - Narrative of Operations 21st to 30th March 1918]
	21/03	05:05	Received order "Man Battle Stations".
		05:15	The Field Coys. and Pioneers assembled at FLUQUIERES. The Transport moved to Battle

Place	Date	Hour	Summary of Events and Information
			Stations as follows: Pioneers (11th South Lancs) - DURY.
		13:10	Received orders to move the Field Coys. and Pioneers to the Quarry behind AVIATION WOOD.
		20:00	Received orders to move the Field Coys. to AUBIGNY. The Pioneers remained behind AVIATION WOOD under the orders of G.O.C. Division.
		21:45	Received orders to move the transport of the Field Coys. and Pioneers to ESMERY HALLON. [30th Division C.R.E. War Diary]
	21/03		Report on Operations from 21st to 28th March 1918 (inclusive) attached hereto.
			Casualties incurred during the month as under -
			Officers - 2nd Lieut. J.P. Mallalieu. Wounded 21.3.18 2/Lt. G. Thomson. Wounded. 23.3.18. Capt. H.A. Hodges. Missing believed Killed 22.3.18 2/Lt. H.C. Harvey. Wounded 23.3.18. Lieut. C.R. Featherby. Wounded. 22.3.18. Lieut. N.S. Ramsbottom. Wounded. 27.3.18. Lieut. J.C. Lidgett. Killed. 23.3.18. 2/Lt. A. Knight. Killed. 23.3.18. 2/Lt. A.E. Holman. Wounded. 28.3.18. Lieut. S.W. McLeod-Braggins. Wounded. 28.3.18. 2/Lt. C.R. Tomkinson. Wounded. 28.3.18.
			Other Ranks. Killed. 14. Wounded 195. Wounded & Missing 5. Missing 194. (During Operations) Other Ranks. Wounded 1 on the 17.3.1918.
			[k.i.a. Sjt. 21168 John Aitken, Pte. 20971 Robert Briscoe, Pte. 21789 John Foster, Pte. 20675 Peter Halliwell, L/Cpl. 21474 Harry Lenton, Pte. 22001 Thomas Nicholson, Pte. 29928 Edward Robbins]
	21/03		On the morning of the 21st my Battalion was

Place	Date	Hour	Summary of Events and Information
			situated as follows :-
			One Company at Savvy Wood Dugouts. One Company in Roupy. One Company split up between L'Epine de Dallon - Roupy and the back area.
			In accordance with Divisional Defence Scheme, as soon as enemy artillery fire made it seem probable that an attack was imminent, all Companies proceeded to Fluquieres. The Company in Savvy Wood lost a certain number of men owing to the fact that the enemy put down a heavy barrage of Gas and H.E. Shells. A few men who were working with the R.E.s. in L'Epine de Dallon did not get clear.
		15:00	At 3 o'clock p.m. we were ordered to withdraw from Fluquieres to the quarry behind Aviation Wood. This was done and picquets were posted on the East side of Aviation Wood.
		19:30	About 7.30 p.m. G.S.O. 3 30th Division informed me that I was to be responsible for my own defence. I accordingly took up a line between Hill Wood and Aviation Wood running from F.25.B.3.2. - F.25.D.6.8. - to L.1.b.5.0. - L.1.D.3.2. This line was dug and partially wired.
[Dury]	21/03	04:40	Heavy enemy bombardment started "MAN BATTLE STATIONS" ordered.
		11:25	CRE reports all 11 South Lancashire, 202 Field Company, 2 sections of 200 Field Company and 2 sections of 201 Field Company concentrated at FLUQUIERES.
		12:55	11 South Lancashire and 3 Field Companies ordered to move to QUARRY west of AVIATION WOOD.
		17:15	CRE reports South Lancs Pioneers and Field Companies arrived QUARRY in rear of AVIATION WOOD. [30th Division HQ War Diary]

Place	Date	Hour	Summary of Events and Information
	22/03		I informed G.O.C. 21st Brigade my position and received orders that I was to hold on to the position and if the infantry in front were compelled to withdraw, they would withdraw through me and reform behind.
			The Battalion remained here, with picquets out in front Aviation Wood and one each flank until 6 p.m. on the 22nd.
			About that time two Companies of the 17th. Kings withdrew on to our line and were being placed into position to strengthen our line when orders were received that all troops were to withdraw in an orderly fashion on HAM. At the time we withdrew the enemy was just coming into view on the crest S.E. of Aviation Wood.
			On arrival at Ham I received orders to bivouac at EPPEVILLE.
[Ham]	22/03	09:00	GSO1 informs 21st Brigade that GOC puts Pioneers at their disposal to be used to cover retirement if necessary. They must not be taken into the fight.
		11:30	11th South Lancashire Pioneers arrived ESMERY-HALLON. Billet 42.
		14:00	11th South Lancashire told they would receive definite orders from 21st Brigade whom they should get in touch with at once.
		19:00	Orders issues as follows: 30th Division will withdraw tonight from battlezone and occupy position in and behind the Somme Defences from SOMMETTE EAUCOURT exclusive to CANIZY exclusive. ... 11th South Lancashire to bivouacs at FLAMICOURT Q.2.b. [30th Division HQ War Diary]
	23/03		About 4.30 on the morning of the 23rd. a certain amount of enemy machine gun fire was heard. I received information from small Units of the 36th. Division, T.M. Batteries - R.E.s that

114

Place	Date	Hour	Summary of Events and Information

everybody was retiring, the enemy was in Ham and that the R.E.s. were waiting for the last troops to come through to blow up the bridge over the canal at K.32. b. 1.7. (66D).

I sent one Platoon as a covering party to the R.E.s. at the bridge. 1 Platoon to my front to take up position near the canal N. of Eppeville and one platoon on the left towards Canizy while the remainder of the Battalion had breakfast on the road.

As I had received no orders of any kind and did not know what was happening on either flank or even if it was intended to hold the line of the canal, I sent to the 89th. Brigade at Esmery Hallon for orders. I waited there until 7 a.m. during which time the canal bridge had been blown up and a considerable number of small units had withdrawn down the Ham-Eppeville Road. A number of men of the 23rd. Entrenching Battalion who stated that they were holding the front line also withdrew through us. I accordingly sent the Battalion under Major Champion along the Ham-Eppeville Road to wait at the cross roads at J.33.b.6.2. until I could get further information from the Brigade. Shortly after, I met the G.S.O 1, 20th. Division in a car. I told him the situation as far as I knew it and he informed me that Canizy was being held and that the 30th. Division was supposed to hold the line the canal. I brought the Battalion back and intended getting into trenches which I understood had been dug along the canal bank with my left on Canizy and try and get into touch with somebody on my right.

The head of the Battalion had reached about J.35 central when information was received from some men of the 19th Kings that the enemy had crossed the canal and was coming on.

I then posted two Companies in some trenches

Place	Date	Hour	Summary of Events and Information

on the high ground about J.35.c. to about J.35.d.4. protecting the right flank and one Company on the Railway embankment from J.34.a.6.2. to J.34.b.4.1.

Men of the 19th Kings under Capt. Smith were in trenches from about J.34.b.3.1. to about J.35.c.7.8. The 23rd. Entrenching Battalion were also holding trenches and part of the Railway towards Canizy but for a considerable time I had no exact knowledge as to where they were.

I was not in touch with anyone on my right.

I then sent out a patrol to reconnoitre the Eppeville-Ham Road as far as the cross roads at K.31.b.8 This patrol reported no signs of the enemy. I accordingly sent out two companies to hold the line of the Railway from J.35.b.4.0. to J.36.d.3.7. with orders to send out a patrol to try and get in touch with someone on our right. About 10 a.m. I received information that the enemy appeared to be massing on the north of the canal and then until about 12.30 there was a considerable number of the enemy moving about in the wood J.29. and J.30. and fairly heavy rifle fire. The enemy appeared to have intended to attack but did not succeed in reaching our line.

About 2 p.m. the 182nd Brigade was seen advancing from our left in the direction of Verlane. They informed me that they intended to attack Verlane, which I knew to be unoccupied by the enemy and to proceed in a north-easterly direction towards Ham.

Just previously, my right Company on the Railway Embankment observed the enemy advancing in south-westerly direction on their right rear. As the Company Commander had failed to get in touch with anyone on his right and as the enemy was on three sides of him, both Companies withdrew to their former positions.

Place	Date	Hour	Summary of Events and Information
			About 6 p.m. I met the O.C. 182nd. Brigade, the O.C. 23rd. Entrenching Battalion and the O.C. of composite Battalion which was on the left of the 182nd Brigade and we arranged to reorganize so to hold a consecutive line. The O.C. Composite Battalion stated that he was holding a line with his left on the Sucrerie at K.31.a.3.2. It afterwards proved that he did not know where his line was and as a matter of fact his left was about 500 yards in rear of it.
			I arranged to get in touch with him with my right flank that night at the Sucrerie which turned out be held by the enemy and the Officer was either killed or captured. At the same time heavy enemy machine gun fire was directed on us from the right flank straight down the Railway line. The enemy also sent up the S.O.S. and turned his Artillery and Trench Mortars on to the Railway cutting. When things became quiet I went to the O.C. 182nd. Brigade and informed him what had happened.
			[k.i.a. Pte. 10213 Albert Asman, Pte. 21097 Thomas Barclay, L/Sjt. 20567 William Gladstone, Pte. 32641 James Boore, Pte. 21334 William Carroll, Pte. 32627 Charles Chamberlain, Pte. 21453 William Clarke, Pte. 21205 Joseph Critchley, Pte. 21392 George Crook, Pte. 22361 Norman Dakin, Cpl. 20001 Robert Davies, Pte. 20542 Henry Elliott, L/Cpl. 20089 John Frodsham, Pte. 20315 Edward Glover, Pte. 266342 James Halmshaw, Pte. 28744 Thomas Handforth, L/Cpl. 20892 David Hughes, Pte. 20153 John Hughes, Cpl. 21243 Richard Kinder, Lt. John Lidgett, Pte. 266155 Sidney Taylor, Sjt. 20511 Joseph Topping]
[Ercheu]	23/03	08:00	Orders for 11th South Lancashire to be attached to Brigades: HQ and 2 companies to 89th Brigade. 1 company each to 21st and 90th Brigades.

Place	Date	Hour	Summary of Events and Information
		11:25	XVIII Corps notified that 11th South Lancashire are holding a good line between J.35.a.0.1 and J.36.d.8.2.
		12:35	90th Brigade report 23rd Entrenching Battalion, 11th South Lancashire and details of Kings still in front of VERLAINES. [30th Division HQ War Diary]
	24/03		The O.C. 23rd. Entrenching Battalion could not be found until 5 o'clock in the morning when he admitted that he had made a mistake as to his front line.

As it was then too late to dig a new line back to the Composite Battalion position and as my position would have been untenable in daylight, I arranged with the O.C. 182nd Brigade to withdraw to my old position and to have some men in support in case the enemy came through the gap between our right and the Composite Battalion's left. About 7 a.m. I saw men of the 23rd. Entrenching Battalion withdrawing from the direction of Canizy. I at once sent orders to the Company in reserve to come up but before they could get into position the troops were falling back on both flanks. The two Companies who were holding the line J.35.c & d. were almost entirely surrounded, their only line withdrawal was across the stream in J.35.c which was lined with barbed wire. Owing to the magnificent way in which the Lewis Gunners remained firing at the enemy until they were either killed or wounded, parts of the two Companies withdrew and fought a rearguard action, across the canal near Moyencourt, where they held trenches.

Meanwhile Battalion H.Qrs. were compelled to withdraw and attempted to find the Company in reserve. This proved impossible owing to the large number of troops retiring. A number of these men were reformed and acted as a covering party to various batteries in turn. When about 1 kilo.

118

Place	Date	Hour	Summary of Events and Information

East of Libermont, I met General Goodman who told me to take up a position there. This was held from 12 noon until about 6.30 p.m. when I received orders to withdraw through the French and take up a line in rear of the Division, between Moyencourt and Cressy. On arrival I reported to the 189th. Brigade and was ordered to hand over the men to their Units and report to Divisional H.Qrs. The reserve Company had fought a rearguard action to Moyencourt when it joined up with the remainder of the Battalion. Major Champion attempted to join up with the reserve company on his left but when about 100 yards from them discovered that it was the enemy and not the reserve Company that he was approaching. The Companies were mixed up with other Units largely Y.C.Vs. who retired in S.W. direction but fell back gradually towards Ramecourt. When a little N.W. of Esmery Hallon, General Williams rode up. The enemy were then nearly 1000 yards away and there was no difficulty in stopping their advance straight ahead. Owing to troops on right or left continually withdrawing, however, it was impossible to stay in our position indefinitely. A battery was covered while it withdrew (A 92) and a point level with Esmery Hallon held about 11 a.m. Ramecourt bridge was crossed at 1 p.m., a Staff Captain riding out and telling us to come back over the bridge. The Battalion was then collected and reported to Lt. Col. Rolle who had command of the defences. We were ordered to Roieglise about 10 p.m. getting there at 5 a.m. 25th.

[d.o.w. Pte. 32601 Benjamin Jacobs]

| [Ercheu /
Solente] | 24/03 | 01:24 | 11th South Lancashire report that they are holding front line from J.35.b.4.1. to K.31.a.3.3. and are not therefore complying with [Operation Order] G.367. |
| | | 07:25 | 61st Division inform that a Pioneer Battalion of |

Place	Date	Hour	Summary of Events and Information
			61st Division will relieve composite force of surplus personnel in front of VERLAINES. 61st Division informed no objection provided relief carried out by daylight. (n.b. see battalion position on previous day.)
		12:30	11th South Lancashire holding out East of LIBERMONT.
		17:10	Warning Order to three brigades and 11th South Lancashire. (1) French will take over this (30th) Division's Front Line from LANNOY Farm inclusive to LIBERMONT bridge. (2) 30th Division will take over line from LANNOY Farm exclusive to BUVERCHY bridge inclusive. [30th Division HQ War Diary]
	24/03	16:00	Reports from Units show total estimated casualties to be 131 Officers 4300 Other Ranks. [30th Division A&Q War Diary]
	25/03		On the 25th Battalion withdrew to Roieglise. During the day I was ordered to take command of a Divisional Composite Battalion. At 5 p.m. the Composite Battalion was ordered to proceed to Plessier where it was billeted at 1 a.m. 25th.
			[d. Pte. 43332 John Roberts; d.o.w. Pte. 20989 John Jones; k.i.a. L/Cpl. 20795 William Atherton]
[Solente / Roiglise]	25/03	10:15	Situation at 10 am. Our front held from BUVERCHY crossing to LANNOY Farm crossing. Light enemy attacks driven off. Both our flanks in close touch with flank divisions. Guns in action about ERCHEU. R.E. digging a line on Eastern outskirts of OMENCOURT and SOLENTE.
		16:35	Composite Battalion under Col. Fenn to march as soon as possible to PLESSIER.
		20:20	Orders issued to all concerned that the Division would withdraw to an area around HANGEST-EN SANTERRE. 11th South Lancashire to PLESSIER.

Place	Date	Hour	Summary of Events and Information
			[30th Division HQ War Diary]
	26/03		At 10 a.m. on the 26th I was ordered to proceed with the Composite Batt. to take up a line between Rouvroy inclusive to le Quesnel returning as many men as possible to their Units on the march. All men of other Units were handed over. On arrival at the Rouvroy-Bouchoir Road I met G.O.C. 89th. Brigade who ordered me to take up a line in some old trenches with my left in front of Rouvroy and informed me that the 19th. Kings would come in on my right when they arrived. This was completed about 2 p.m. I was then in touch on my left with a battalion of the Royal Warwickshire Regt.
			Shortly after, the Warwicks withdrew from the line. I reported to 89th. Brigade and 150 men of 17th K.L.R. were sent to hold the line in front of Rouvroy at about 8 p.m. At 11 p.m. O.C. 17th K.L.R. reported they were in touch on their left.
			As a number of old communication trenches ran back from the enemy to my front line I had them filled in for 100 yards in front.
[Hangest-en-Santerre]	26/03	08:50	Patrols were sent out about 1000 yards in front and got in touch with the enemy over the crest, at 4 p.m. Patrolling carried on all night. Orders issued to all concerned as follows: 30th Division will take up a line which will be pointed out by Staff Officers from ROUVROY (6 miles NW of ROYE) to Le QUESNOY inclusive southward with strong points on AMIENS-ROYE road. Officers to proceed at once and reconnoitre line. Troops to be got moving at once. 11th South Lancashire to be attached to 89th Brigade.
		17:40	30th Division Order No. 160 issued. Dispositions: 30th Division will hold a defensive position about BOUCHOIRE and ROUVROY and along the road joining these two villages with a strong point

Place	Date	Hour	Summary of Events and Information
			on the main ROYE-AMIENS road at BUCHOIRE. [90th Brigade on right, 89th Brigade on left, 21st Brigade in reserve]. Intention: The GOC intends to delay the enemy as long as possible. Present positions must be held at all costs. [30th Division HQ War Diary]
	27/03		At 9 a.m. on the 27th men of the 17th Kings commenced to move to their right along my front line they were ordered to return to their trenches which they did. About 10 a.m. the 17th K.L.R. withdrew behind Houvroy without informing me of their intention. I heard that the troops on their left had also withdrawn. I ordered my left Company to form a defensive flank and reported to the 89th Brigade. I consulted with Lt. Col. Rollo and we decided that we could hold on but wanted supports sent up on our left as enemy snipers had by then occupied Rouvroy and were enfilading trenches. At about 10.45 a.m. I received orders from Brigade by telephone to withdraw on a line Hangest Flessier. I understood that troops on right of Divisional line had also withdrawn.
			The 19th K.L.R. and 11th South Lancs then withdrew in extended order giving each other cover fire until they reached a point S. of Folies where they got into Artillery formation, and withdrew as far as the quarry on the Roye-Amiens Road, W. of Folies.
			The rearguard again got into touch with the 17th K.L.R. due W. of Rouvroy. The officer in charge was ordered by the brigade Major 72nd. Brigade to hold on there, which he did until the 61st.
			Division had dug in just in rear of him. He then rejoined the Battalion at about 8 p.m.
			At the Quarry was met by a Colonel on horseback who said the withdrawal was due to a mistake. Then reformed my Battalion into extended order

Place	Date	Hour	Summary of Events and Information
			and counter-attacked together with the 2nd R.S.F 2nd Bedfords, 19th K.L.R., and a Battalion of Manchesters on the left.
			We advanced to a line running in front of Folies and along road from Folies towards Arvillers, where we were held up by Machine Gun and Trench mortar fire from Arvillers and Souchoir. We then occupied an old trench with a few men on the road in front. I consulted with Colonel Kelso, R.S.F and Major Wynn of the Befords and as the trench was too packed with men, we decided to reorganize at dusk. Bedfords to hold the right in touch with some Manchesters. South Lancs to dig support line 300 yards in rear with 19th K.L.R. in reserve, already dug in 400 yards in rear again.
			[k.i.a. Pte. 20372 James Burrows, C.S.M. 21019 Matthew Carroll, L/Cpl. 20885 John Griffiths, Pte. 266523 John Lewis, Pte. 20333 William McConnell, Pte. 45132 Alexander Robertson, Pte. 336570 Albert Smith, Pte. 22039 Isaac Whelan]
[Hangest-en-Santerre / Braches]	27/03	10:55 11:20	Various reports received that troops are retiring on both flanks of the Division and that some of our troops are commencing to retire.
		12:45	90th Brigade report line still holding but men are rather shaken.
		20:20	Divisional Order No. 161 issued at 8.20 pm. 30th Division to be relieved in the line tonight by 113rd Division (French). No time can be fixed for the relief which will probably take place at a late hour. As soon as British units are relieved by the corresponding French units the former will be withdrawn to a place of rendezvous to be appointed by Brigadiers. No British units will withdraw from the forward zone until they have been properly relieved. From the places of rendezvous units will march to bivouacs or billets. ..... 89th Brigade to bivouac on HANGEST-

Place	Date	Hour	Summary of Events and Information
			PLESSIER road just W of HANGEST. Brigadiers will arrange relief of all units attached to or else in close contact with their own units and all commanders will make every effort to see that no portion of our troops are behind ..... Cookers and watercarts will be sent to the bivouacs detailed above. Divisional HQ is BRACHES. [30th Division HQ War Diary]
	28/03		On the morning of the 28th the enemy commenced to shell our positions, it became necessary to remove some of the men in the support line to the left flank.
			At 11.30 a.m. the R.I.R. on the right flank withdrew under orders of an Officer of that Regiment. I sent one Company across the road to defend the flank. By 12.15 p.m. all R.I.R. on right flank had withdrawn. It became necessary to send all the 11th South Lancs and some of the 19th K.L.R. on the flank in order to keep the enemy from debouching from Arvillers. This was successfully done.
			1.30 p.m. I was informed by 89th. Brigade that the French had relieved us and that we were to withdraw through them. I arranged with Col. Rollo and Col. Kelso that we would hold the flank until the troops in the front line had withdrawn. This was successfully accomplished.
			The Battalion then withdrew to Rouvrel.
			[d.o.w. Pte. 21847 James Burgess, Pte. 22357 Joseph Collins, Pte. 21679 Lawrence Hannon, Pte 20909 Thomas Mather, Pte. 22023 Michael McCarthy; k.i.a. Pte. 20143 James Chisnall, Pte. 21753 Henry Deacle, Pte. 20359 Matthew Houghton, Pte. 21024 Hugh Jones, Pte. 21104 Joseph Ratcliffe, Pte. 21472 Edward Rigby, Pte. 20322 Joseph Wilkinson, Pte. 21664 Thomas Wylie]

Place	Date	Hour	Summary of Events and Information
[Braches / Estrees]	28/03	09:00	90th Brigade report still in line E of FOLIES and have not yet been relieved by French.
		10:00	90th Brigade report enemy shelling front line heavily.
		22:30	Message sent to XVIII Corps as follows. Division handed over the line from main AMIENS Road north and east of FOLIES now firmly held to the French at 1.30 pm today. All enemy attacks from noon yesterday had been repulsed with severe loss to the enemy. Division is now concentrated at ROUVREL. Infantry brigades average 500 strong. [30th Division HQ War Diary]
	29/03		[d. Pte. 21630 John Pye; d.o.w. Pte. 21892 Michael Cooney, L/Sjt. 20043 Frederick Pendlebury; k.i.a. C.S.M. 240010 Herbert Boyer]
[Estrees]	29/03	13:30	Strength of Division reported to be 21st Brigade 450, 89th Brigade 1,000, 90th Brigade 500 and 1 machine guns. Division temporarily organised as one brigade, each brigade making one composite battalion, the whole of the infantry being under the command of General Stevens. [30th Division HQ War Diary]
	30/03		The Battalion entrained at SALEUX for VALERY-Sur-SOMME. On the 31st March Battalion located at LANCHIERES, near VALERY-Sur-SOMME.
Lanchieres	31/03		The Battalion located as reported in the last portion of the War Diary for the month of March 1918 viz. LANCHIERES, Nr. Valery-sur-Somme.

[d.o.w. L/Cpl. 20099 John Batten]

CASUALTIES FROM 21st MARCH to 31st MARCH 1918

11th South Lancs. Regt.		Killed	Wounded	Missing	Total
	Officers	2	9	1	12
	O.R.	15	193	188	396
	Total	18	202	189	408

[30th Division A&Q War Diary]

REPORT ON OPERATIONS FROM 21st. to 28th. MARCH 1918.

21st. On the morning of the 21st my Battalion was situated as follows:-

> One Company at Savvy Wood Dugouts.
> One Company in Roupy.
> One Company split up between L'Epine de Dallon - Roupy and the back area.

In accordance with Divisional Defence Scheme, as soon as enemy artillery fire made it seem probable that an attack was imminent, all Companies proceeded to Fluquieres. The Company in Savvy Wood lost a certain number of men owing to the fact that the enemy put down a heavy barrage of Gas and H.E. Shells. A few men who were working with the R.E.s. in L'Epine de Dallon did not get clear.

At 3 o'clock p.m. we were ordered to withdraw from Fluquieres to the quarry behind Aviation Wood. This was done and picquets were posted on the East side of Aviation Wood.

About 7.30 p.m. G.S.O. 3 30th Division informed me that I was to be responsible for my own defence. I accordingly took up a line between Hill Wood and Aviation Wood running from F.25.B.3.2. - F.25.D.6.8. - to L.1.b.5.0. - L.1.D.3.2. This line was dug and partially wired.

22nd.

I informed G.O.C. 21st Brigade my position and received orders to that I was to hold on to the position and if the infantry in front were compelled to withdraw, they would withdraw through me and reform behind.

The Battalion remained here, with picquets out in front Aviation Wood and one each flank until 6 p.m. on the 22nd.

About that time two Companies of the 17th. Kings withdrew on to our line and were being placed into position to strengthen our line when orders were received that all troops were to withdraw in an orderly fashion on HAM. At the time we withdrew the enemy was just coming into view on the crest S.E. of Aviation Wood.

On arrival at Ham I received orders to bivouac at EPPEVILLE.

23rd.

About 4.30 on the morning of the 23rd. a certain amount of enemy machine gun fire was heard. I received information from small Units of the 36th. Division, T.M. Batteries - R.E.s that everybody was retiring, the enemy was in Ham and that the R.E.s. were waiting for the last troops to come through to blow up the bridge over the canal at K.32. b. 1.7. (66D)

I sent one Platoon as a covering party to the R.E.s. at the bridge. 1 Platoon to my front to take up position near the canal N. of Eppeville and one platoon on the left towards Canizy while the remainder of the Battalion had breakfast on the road.

As I had received no orders of any kind and did not know what was happening on either flank or even if it was intended to hold the line of the canal, I sent to the 89th. Brigade at Esmery Hallon for orders. I waited there until 7 a.m. during which time the canal bridge had been blown up and a considerable number of small units had withdrawn down the Ham-Eppeville Road. A number of men of the 23rd. Entrenching Battalion who stated that they were holding the front line also withdrew through us. I accordingly sent the Battalion under Major Champion along the Ham-Eppeville Road to wait at the cross roads at J.33.b.6.2. until I could get further information from the Brigade. Shortly after, I met the G.S.O 1, 20th. Division in a car. I told him the situation as far as I knew it and he informed me that Canizy was being held and that the 30th. Division was supposed to hold the line of the canal. I brought the Battalion back and intended getting into trenches which I understood had been dug along the canal bank with my left on Canizy and try and get into touch with somebody on my right.

The head of the Battalion had reached about J.35 central when information was received from some men of the 19th. Kings that the enemy had crossed the canal and was coming on.

I then posted two Companies in some trenches on the high ground about J.35.c. to about J.35.d.4.7., protecting the right flank and one Company on the Railway embankment from J.34.a.6.2. to J.34.b.4.1.

Men of the 19th Kings under Capt. Smith were in trenches from about J.34.b.3.1. to about J.35.c.7.8. The 23rd Entrenching Battalion were also holding trenches and part of the Railway towards Canizy but for a considerable time I had no exact knowledge as to where they were.

I was not in touch with anyone on my right.

I then sent out a patrol to reconnoitre the Eppeville-Ham Road as far as the cross roads at K.31.b.8.0. This patrol reported no signs of the enemy. I accordingly sent out two companies to hold the line of the Railway from J.35.b.4.0. to J.36.d.3.7. with orders to send out a patrol to try and get in touch with someone on our right. About 10 a.m. I received information that the enemy appeared to be massing on the north of the canal and then until about 12.30 there was a considerable number of the enemy moving about in the wood

J.29. and J.30. and fairly heavy rifle fire. The enemy appeared to have intended to attack but did not succeed in reaching our line.

About 2 p.m. the 182nd. Brigade was seen advancing from our left in the direction of Verlane. They informed me that they intended to attack Verlaine, which I knew to be unoccupied by the enemy and to proceed in a north-easterly direction towards Ham.

Just previously, my right Company on the Railway Embankment observed the enemy advancing in a south-westerly direction on their right rear. As the Company Commander had failed to get in touch with anyone on his right and as the enemy was on three sides of him, both Companies withdrew to their former positions.

About 6 p.m. I met the O.C. 182nd Brigade, the O.C. 23rd Entrenching Battalion and the O.C. of a composite Battalion which was on the left of the 182nd. Brigade and we arranged to reorganize so as to hold a consecutive line. The O.C. Composite Battalion stated that he was holding a line with his left on the Sucrerie at K.31.a.3.2. It afterwards proved that he did not know where his line was and as a matter of fact his left was about 500 yards in rear of it.

I arranged to get in touch with him with my right flank that night at the Sucrerie which turned out to be held by the enemy and the Officer was either killed or captured. At the same time heavy enemy machine gun fire was directed on us from the right flank straight down the Railway line. The enemy also sent up the S.O.S. and turned his Artillery and Trench Mortars on to the Railway cutting. When things became quiet I went to the O.C. 182nd. Brigade and informed him what had happened.

24th.

The O.C. 23rd Entrenching Battalion could not be found until 5 o'clock in the morning when he admitted that he had made a mistake as to his front line.

As it was then too late to dig a new line back to the Composite Battalion position and as my position would have been untenable in daylight, I arranged with the O.C. 182nd Brigade to withdraw to my old position and to have some men in support in case the enemy came through the gap between our right and the Composite Battalion's left. About 7 a.m. I saw men of the 23rd Entrenching Battalion withdrawing from the direction of Canizy. I at once sent orders to the Company in reserve to come up but before they could get into position the troops were falling back on both flanks. The two Companies who were holding the line J.35.c & d. were almost entirely surrounded, their only line of withdrawal was across the stream in J.35.c. which was lined with barbed wire. Owing to the magnificent way in which the Lewis Gunners remained firing at the enemy until they were either killed or wounded, parts of the two Companies withdrew and fought a rearguard action, across the canal near Moyencourt, where they held trenches.

Meanwhile Battalion H.Qrs. Were compelled to withdraw and attempted to find the Company in reserve. This proved impossible owing to the large number of troops retiring. A number of these men were reformed and acted as a covering party to various batteries in turn. When about 1 kilo. East of Libermont, I met General Goodman who told me to take up a position there. This was held from 12 noon until about 6.30 p.m. when I received orders to withdraw through the French and take up a line in rear of the Division, between Moyencourt and Cressy. On arrival I reported to the 189th. Brigade and was ordered to hand over the men to their Units and report to Divisional H.Qrs. The reserve Company had fought a rearguard action to Moyencourt when it joined up with the remainder of the Battalion. Major Champion attempted to join up with the reserve company on his left but when about 100 yards from them discovered that it was the enemy and not the reserve Company that he was approaching. The Companies were mixed up with other Units largely Y.C.Vs. who retired in a S.W. direction but fell back gradually towards Ramecourt. When a little N.W. of Esmery Hallon, General Williams rode up. The enemy were then nearly 1000 yards away and there was no difficulty in stopping their advance straight ahead. Owing to troops on right or left continually withdrawing, however, it was impossible to stay in our position indefinitely. A battery was covered while it withdrew (A 92) and a point level with Esmery Hallon held about 11 a.m. Ramecourt bridge was crossed at 1 p.m., a Staff Captain riding out and telling us to come back over the bridge. The Battalion was then collected and reported to Lt. Col. Rolle who had command of the defences. We were ordered to Roiglise about 10 p.m. getting there at 5 a.m. 25th.

25th.

On the 25th Battalion withdrew to Roiglise. During the day I was ordered to take command of a Divisional Composite Battalion. At 5 p.m. the Composite Battalion was ordered to proceed to Plessier where it was billeted at 1 a.m. 25th.

26th.

At 10 a.m. on the 26th I was ordered to proceed with the Composite Batt. to take up a line between Rouvroy inclusive to le Quesnel returning as many men as possible to their Units on the march. All men of other Units were handed over. On arrival at the Rouvroy-Bouchoir Road I met G.O.C. 89th Brigade who ordered me to take up a line in some old trenches with my left in front of Rouvroy and informed me that the 19th Kings would come in on my right when they arrived. This was completed about 2 p.m. I was then in touch on my left with a battalion of the Royal Warwickshire Regt.

Shortly after, the Warwicks withdrew from the line. I reported to 89th Brigade and 150 men of 17th K.L.R. were sent to hold the line in front of Rouvroy at about 8 p.m. At 11 p.m. O.C. 17th K.L.R. reported they were in touch on their left.

As a number of old communication trenches ran back from the enemy to my front line I had them filled in for 100 yards in front.

Patrols were sent out about 1000 yards in front and got in touch with the enemy over the crest, at 4 p.m. Patrolling carried on all night.

27th.

At 9 a.m. on the 27th men of the 17th Kings commenced to move to their right along my front line, they were ordered to return to their trenches which they did. About 10 a.m. the 17th K.L.R. withdrew behind Rouvroy without informing me of their intention. I heard that the troops on their left had also withdrawn. I ordered my left Company to form a defensive flank and reported to the 89th Brigade. I consulted with Lt. Col. Rollo and we decided that we could hold on but wanted supports sent up on our left as enemy snipers had by then occupied Rouvroy and were enfilading my trenches. At about 10.45 a.m. I received orders from Brigade by telephone to withdraw on a line Hangest Flessier. I understood that troops on right of Divisional line had also withdrawn.

The 19th K.L.R. and 11th South Lancs. then withdrew in extended order giving each other covering fire until they reached a point S. of Folies where they got into Artillery formation, and withdrew as far as the quarry on the Roye-Amiens Road, W. of Folies.

The rearguard again got into touch with the 17th K.L.R. due W. of Rouvroy. The officer in charge was ordered by the brigade Major 72nd Brigade to hold on there, which he did until the 61st Division had dug in just in rear of him. He then rejoined the Battalion at about 8 p.m.

At the Quarry was met by a Colonel on horseback who said the withdrawal was due to a mistake. I then reformed my Battalion into extended order and counter-attacked together with the 2nd R.S.F. 2nd Bedfords, 19th K.L.R., and a Battalion of Manchesters on the left.

We advanced to a line running in front of Folies and along road from Folies towards Arvillers, where we were held up by Machine Gun and Trench mortar fire from Arvillers and Souchoir. We then occupied an old trench with a few men on the road in front. I consulted with Colonel Kelso, R.S.F., and Major Wynn of the Bedfords and as the trench was too packed with men, we decided to reorganize at dusk. Bedfords to hold the right in touch with some

Manchesters. South Lancs. to dig a support line 300 yards in rear with 19th K.L.R. in reserve, already dug in 400 yards in rear again.

28th.

On the morning of the 28th the enemy commenced to shell our positions, it became necessary to remove some of the men in the support line to the left flank.

At 11.30 a.m. the R.I.R. on the right flank withdrew under orders of an Officer of that Regiment. I sent one Company across the road to defend the flank. By 12.15 p.m. all R.I.R. on right flank had withdrawn. It became necessary to send all the 11th South Lancs. and some of the 19th K.L.R. on the flank in order to keep the enemy from debouching from Arvillers. This was successfully done. At 1.30 p.m. I was informed by 89th Brigade that the French had relieved us and that we were to withdraw through them. I arranged with Col. Rollo and Col. Kelso that we would hold the flank until the troops in the front line had withdrawn. This was successfully accomplished.

The Battalion then withdrew to Rouvrel.

H F Fenn Lieut.Col.
Comdg. 11th. South Lancashire Regt.
(Pioneers)

2.4.18

Place	Date	Hour	Summary of Events and Information
	03/04		[d.o.w. Pte. 20532 William Pye]
	04/04		[d.o.w. Pte. 20930 George Lees]
	05/04		At midnight the battalion marched to FOUQUIERES, there entraining at 6 a.m. and detraining at ROESBRUGGE at 9 p.m. From detraining station conveyed by Lorries to YORK CAMP, N.W. o Poperinghe.
			[d.ow. - Pte. 22399 Frederick Thomason]
	07/04		Battalion marched from York Camp to TURCO CAMP, N.E. of YPRES (Sh.28/C.15.c) Transport located at OTTER CAMP A.12.a.1.5. (Sh.28)
			Battalion relieved the 1st Division Pioneer Battn. and took over work on Duckboard Tracks and Roads in front of the STEENBEEK and within Divisional Boundaries.
	08/04		[d.o.w. Pte. 21131 Thomas Webster]
	09/04		[d.o.w. Pte. 32629 Thomas Goddard]
	10/04		On the 10.4.18 all Coys paraded as strong as possible for work on the wiring of the BATTLE ZONE.
	11/04		1 Coy continued work on roads, 1 Coy work on Tracks, and 1 Coy work on Forward Posts.
			[d.o.w. Pte. 20416 James Kay]
	13/04		[d.o.w. Pte. 43569 Richard Griffiths]
	16/04		Battalion moved to LOCHAEL CAMP (Sh.28. B.15.c.9.2.) Coys moving to this Camp after completion of work on Strong Points and Battle Zone area.
			[d. Pte. 240176 Walter Wright; d.o.w. Pte. 20682 George McKie]
	18/04		Battalion moved by march route under orders of 21st Inf. Brigade to Camp situated at G.23.c.6.4. Nr. RENINGHELST.
	18/04		Field Companies and 11th South Lancs Regt.

Place	Date	Hour	Summary of Events and Information
			(Pioneers) moved to BRANDHOEK - BUSSEBOOM area and took over work on the DRANOUTRE - OUDERDOM (3rd Reserve) Line. [30th Division C.R.E. War Diary]
	18/04		11th Bn. South Lancs Regt. (Pioneers) and 1 Battalion Infantry on Intermediate Posts at H.8.c.6.0, H.14.d.0.2., H.15.c.6.9 and H.26.c.2.8. [30th Division C.R.E. War Diary]
	19/04		Coys working on, on the Strong Points situated Nr. Ouderdom until 25.4.18 when Battalion was ordered to remain in Camp and be prepared to move at half hour's notice. No work was carried out on 25.4.18 due to the enemy heavy bombardment and subsequent attacks. At 3 p.m. received order to move at once to LAWRENCE CAMP G.11.c.6.5. (Sh.28)
	23/04		[d.o.w. Pte. 21056 Peter Grumley, Pte. 43398 William McMahon]
	25/04		Work carried on, on the Strong Points Nr. Ouderdom until the 25.4.18 when Battalion was ordered to remain in Camp and be prepared to move at half hour's notice. No work was carried out on 25.4.18 due to the enemy heavy bombardment and subsequent attacks. At 3 p.m. received orders to move at once to LAWRENCE CAMP G.11.c.6.5. (Sh. 28)
	26/04		[d.o.w. Pte. 21659 Horace Boardman]
	27/04		Battalion attached to the C.R.E. 49th Division for work on and from 6 a.m. 27.4.18.
	28/04		Battalion moved to L.23.c.9.9. (Sh. 27) and prepared camp for occupation, Coys joining B.H.Q. after completion of work on Forward roads that day.
			On the 28.4.18. Major C.C. Champion. D.S.O. was Invalided to England.

Place	Date	Hour	Summary of Events and Information
			Captain J.E.S. Pethick M.C., took over the duties of 2nd in Command on the 14.4.18 the date on which Major C.C. Champion was admitted to Hospital.
			Acting Rank of Major given to Captain J.E.S. Pethick M.C. with effect from 29.4.18.
	30/04		Work continued on Forward roads under the orders of C.R.E. 49th Division.
			Battalion located at L.23.c.9.9., with Transport at L.21.d.5.6.
			The undermentioned Officers, W.O. and men were awarded honours as shewn for gallantry in action during the heavy fighting and withdrawal on the ST.QUENTIN front in March 1918.

Major. C. C. Champion. D.S.O.
Capt. J.E.S. Pethick. M.C.
2nd Lieut. J.J. Acton. M.C.
Lieut. S.E. Boulton. M.C.

No.20581 R.S.M. J. Harrington. M.C., D.C.M.
No.22007 Sergt. W. Twinning. D.C.M.
No.20818 Sergt. H. Sandford. M.M.
No.20280 L/C. Milligan A.M. M.M.
No.21043 Pte. W. Seaton. M.M.
No.20377 Pte. Prescott J. M.M.
No.21479 Pte. J. Percival. M.M.
No.21612 Pte. Jones T. M.M.
No.20813 Sgt. J. Taylor. M.M.
No.21132 Pte. A. Atherton. M.M.

No.20569 Cpl. (L/Sgt) Blake W. M.M., Bar to Military Medal.

Strength of Battalion on the 30.4.1918 :
23 Officers. 494 Other Ranks.

The casualties incurred during March 1918 as under, and cancel those shewn in War Diary for March 1918 which were not complete as regards verification with the Hospital Sheets the latter not

Place	Date	Hour	Summary of Events and Information
			having been received at time of forwarding War Diary. Officers casualties as shewn in last Diary - Other Ranks. Killed 14. Wounded. 149. Wounded and Missing. 34. Missing. 176. Died of Wounds. 14. Wounded and since rejoined 20.
			Major G.F. Beal, and 2nd Lieut. A. Hughes have both been struck off the strength of Battn during the month, having been invalided to England in the case of the latter Officer, and Major G.F. Beal unfit to return from leave, and Medical Board ordered by War Office.
			H F Fenn Lieut. Colonel. Comdg. 11th (S) Bn. S. Lancashire Regt. (Pioneers).
L.23.c.9.9. (Sheet 27)	01/05		Battalion located a t L.23.c.9.9. as shewn in last month's Diary, with Transport at L.21.d.5.6.
			Continued work on forward roads under orders of C.R.E. 49th Division.
	03/05		Lieut. W. Bretherton and Lieut. C.H.N. Symon reported to Battn. for duty after a tour of light duty for 6 months in England.
	05/05		Changed location on the 5th inst. and moved to new Camp near St. Jan-ter-Biezen.
			Work continued on the OUDERDOM SWITCH Line, under 33 Divn parties being conveyed to sit of work by train.
	09/05		Captain A.T. Champion, and Capt. C.J. Dixon M.C. reported to Battn. for duty after a tour of light duty for 6 months in England.
	10/05		Battn. moved by Bus to the LEDERZEELE Area, and located in Billets in vicinity of B.28.a & b (Sheet 27) Instructions received that the Battalion was to be broken up, all surplus Officers and Other Ranks over and above establishment of 10 Officers and 51 O.R.s being disposed of as under.

Place	Date	Hour	Summary of Events and Information
	11/05		Authority received for Capt. A.T. Champion and Lieut. S.E. Boulton M.C. to wear the badges of the rank of Major and Captain respectively, pending notification in the London Gazette.
	12/05		301 Other Ranks transferred to the 19th Bn. Lancashire Fusiliers.
			300 Other Ranks transferred from the 19th Lancs Fusiliers to this Battn.
			[d. L/Cpl. 22137 Frederick Marsh]
	13/05		30 Other Ranks proceeded with the Battalion Transport, less Officers Mess Cart, 1 Water Cart, and 1 A.S.C. Supply Wagon, to the 30th Div. Transport Concentration Camp, CUC.
	14/05		381 Other Ranks and 7 Officers (names as under) transferred to the Base Camp, ETAPLES for disposal as reinforcements to other Units.
			Officers - Captain A.T. Champion. Capt. R.G. Dunthorne. Lieut. W. Bretherton. Lieut. C.H.N. Symon. Lieut. B.F. Mackenzie. 2nd Lt. A.D. Hurley. 2nd lieut. K.N. Harpur.
			[d.o.w. L/Sjt. 20984 James Flanagan]
	15/05		Lt. Colonel H.F. Fenn, D.S.O. ordered to proceed to take over Command of the 19th Bn. Lancashire Fusiliers.
			The remainder of the Battalion, known now as the Battalion Training Cadre, for an American Battalion, received orders to move on the 15.5.18 to EU Training Area.
			Proceeded by March route to AUDRUICQ there entraining for WOINCOURT Railhead. Bn. Training Cadre located at BEAUMONT CHATEAU, Nr. EU.
			Major J.E.S. Pethick M.C. took over Command of the Battn Training Cadre, on Lt. Colonel H.F. Fenn. D.S.O. being ordered to proceed and take

Place	Date	Hour	Summary of Events and Information
			over Command of the 19th Bn. Lancashire Fusiliers.
	16/05		[d. Pte. 235420 Henry Sillitoe; d.o.w. Pte. 235405 Matthew Cadwallader]
	18/05		Capt. C.J. Dixon. M.C. and Lieut. H.M. Fieldhouse appointed Divisional Range Officer and Div. & B.T. Officer respectively, and reported to Div. H.Q. accordingly for duty.
	19/05		Bn. Training Cadre moved from BEAUMONT CHATEAU, to TOUFFREVILLE, where the 110th Engineer Regt. were billeted.
	19/05		Headquarters, 11th South Lancs (Pioneers) Training Cadre established at TOUFFREVILLE. [30th Division C.R.E. War Diary]
	20/05		Commenced Training of the Coys and H.Q. 110th Engineer Regt. in Musketry, Gas & P & B.T. On the 20th May, 1918 the following award appeared in Divisional Routine Orders.

His Majesty the King has been graciously pleased to approve of the grant of the VICTORIA CROSS to No. 20765 CORPORAL J.T. DAVIES, this Battalion, for conspicuous bravery whilst serving in the Expeditionary Force, as set forth below:-

For the greatest courage and devotion to duty under heavy rifle and machine gun fire on March 24th 1918, near EPPEVILLE.

When his Company on being outflanked on both sides received orders to withdraw this N.C.O. knew that the only line of withdrawal lay through a deep stream lined with a belt of barbed wire and that it was imperative to hold up the enemy as long as possible. He mounted the parapet, fully exposing himself, in order to get a more effective field of fire and kept his Lewis Gun in action to last, causing the enemy many casualties and checking their advance.

Place	Date	Hour	Summary of Events and Information
			By his very great devotion to duty he enabled part of his Coy to get across the river which they otherwise would have been unable to do so, thus undoubtedly saving the lives of many of his comrades.
			When last seen he was still firing his Gun with the enemy close on top of him and was in all probability killed at his Gun.
			(Authy. XVIII Corps Wire A/68 dated 19.5.18).
			Information has since been received that Cpl. J.T. Davies is unwounded and a Prisoner of War in Germany.
			J E S Pethick Major. Commanding 11th (S) Bn. S. Lancs Reg. (Pioneers)
	22/05		Musketry and Gas training was started by the Pioneers on a scale of 4 hours Gas & 2 hours musketry instruction per Coy per week. The Coys not being instructed in Gas or Musketry were employed on steady drill, Bombing & physical training. [30th Division C.R.E. War Diary]
	27/05		Orders received to move Training Staff to ARGOEUVES along with the 110th American Engineer Regt. who were to be employed on the construction of a G.H.Q. Line of Defence in rear of AMIENS Area.
			2 Coys per day of the Engineers Regt. at our disposal for Training Purposes, the Staff being divided up in to 2 portions in order to meet the requirements and dispositions of the Coys of American Engineers.
	28/05		[k.i.a. Pte. 17932 William Noble]
	29/05		[d.o.w. Pte. 20030 Thomas Bradbury]
	12/06		The 11th Bn. South Lancs Regt. (Pioneers) Training Cadre will be attached to 108th Engineer

Place	Date	Hour	Summary of Events and Information
			Regt [33rd American Division] in the new area and will assist them in musketry, gas and other training, as may be required. The 11th Bn South Lancs Regt. will be prepared to move from their present camp, so as to be in close touch with 108th Engineer Regiment. [30th Division C.R.E. War Diary]
	19/06		[d.o.w. Pte. 20970 Job Webster]
	28/06		[d. Pte. 266346 James Hornsall]
	10/07		[d. L/Cpl. 20577 Joseph Garner]
	18/07		11th S Lancs proceeded to Eastern Command (North Walsham) [25th Division A&Q War Diary]
	20/07		[d. Pte. 32628 Arthur Dally]
	22/07		[d. L/Cpl. 26414 Robert Sumner]
	21/08		[k.i.a. Pte. 34530 Percival Elliott]
Le Havre	07/10 to 08/10		1/2 Bn arrived at Le Havre from Aldershot.
	10/10		Remainder arrived at Le Havre from Aldershot Area.
			The Battalion on arrival from England was composed mainly of 'B' men & a total of 36 Officers. Marched up to No 1 Rest Camp Le Havre & stayed there until the 10th Oct 1918 in the meantime all ranks were being fitted up with deficiencies in clothing & equipment prior to proceeding up the line.
Roisel	11/10 to 13/10		Battn arrived by Train at ROISEL Railhead & remained under canvas there for the night, moving following day the 12th Oct 1918 by march route for ESTREE staying there the night & proceeding on 13th Oct 1918 by march route for PREMONT. On the 11th Oct 1918 the Battn came under the orders of the 25th Divn to which

139

Place	Date	Hour	Summary of Events and Information
			we were to be Pioneers. The attached is a copy of brief narrative of part taken by Battn in operations from 13th Oct to 31st Oct 1918.
	13/10		The Battalion joined the 25th Division on the 13/10/18 and went into Billets at PREMONT.
			11th S Lancs (Pioneers) joined the Division from England and billeted at PREMONT. Orders issued that strictest attention is to be paid to the sanitation of billets, villages and their surroundings. [25th Division A&Q War Diary]
	14/10		On the 14/10/18 work was carried out by all 3 Coys on Roads in the PREMONT - SERRIN - ELINCOURT Area under the C.R.E. 25th Division.
	15/10		On the 15th inst work was continued on Roads in the above area which consisted of the filling in shell holes, craters, and drainage.

SECRET

OPERATION ORDERS BY LIEUT.COLONEL, R.J..DONE, D.S.O., R.E. C.R.E., 25TH DIVISION.

No. 241   15th, OCTOBER, 1918.

1.   The XIII Corps is going to attack at an early date, probably 17th instant. The XIII Corps Boundaries and objectives are shown on the attached tracing. The 2nd American Corps will co-operate on the right. Possibly the 3rd Army will co-operate on the Left. This is not certain.

2.   The Divisions taking part in the attack, on XIII Corps Front will be 50th Division on the right, and 68th Division on the left. Possibly one Brigade of the 25th Division will be in reserve. Headquarters of 66th Division is in MARETZ, that of 50th Division is at TROU AUX SOLDATS.

3.   For the hasty bridging of the River SELLE, the 50th and 66th Divisions are required to erect permanent road bridges at the following places:-

        No. 1.   K.34.b.1.0.
        No. 2.   K.34.d.0.0.
        No. 3.   O.9.b.4.0.
        No. 4.   O.22.a.2.1.

        The 106th Field Company R.E. will undertake Bridge No. 1, the 130th Field Company R.E. Bridges Nos. 2, and 3 and the 105th Field Company R.E., Bridge No. 4. One Company of 11th South Lancs. (Pioneers) will be detailed to assist.

4.   On the evening of 16/10/18, after dusk, the Field Companies R.E. will move up as follows:-

        106th. Field Coy. R.E.   to neighbourhood of P.17. Central.
        105th. Field Coy. R.E.   to neighbourhood of P.28. Central.
        130th. Field Coy. R.E.   to neighbourhood of P.28. Central.

        One Company of 11th South Lancs. (Pioneers) to neighbourhood of P.17.a.Central.

        Headquarters of these units will remain in present locations. Field Companies will take with them, two double tool-carts and two pontoon wagons each. Pioneer Coys. will require picks, shovels and crowbars.

5.   Within the road loop at P.17.a.8.3. the C.E. XIII Corps is forming a Bridging Park. Captain MURNANE, R.E., 106th Field Coy. R.E. will be in charge of it; with One Section of the 106th Field Coy. R.E. until 17/10/1918. At Zero

Hour on 17/10/1918 a party of 1 N.C.O. and 20 Men of the Pioneer Company will report to R.S.M. WELLER at this Bridging Park, to load lorries, wagons, etc. R.S.M. WELLER, R.E. will work under the orders of Capt. MURNANE, R.E.

Details of Road Bridges are as follows:-

No. 1. (K.34.b.1.2.) Masonry - 26' span - width of roadway 55' 9". Has been blown up.

No. 2. (K.34.d.0.0.) Cast Iron - two spans each 23' - width of roadway 16'6". Destroyed.

No. 3. (O.9.b.4.0.) Masonry - 18' 2" span. This bridge has not been blown up; but has been smashed by shell-fire.

No. 4. (O.22.a.2.1.) Iron - 18' 0" span - width of roadway 9' 9". Has been blown up.

The abutments of No. 3 should be intact; but are probably blown up in the case of Nos. 1, 2 and 4. This is not certain.

6.   Attached list shews material which is being sent up to-day from 4th Army Bridging Depot. In addition, C.E. XIII Corps is sending considerable material from his own stores, to the forward Bridging Depot. Briefly the following Bridges will be available.

1 Bridge 21' 6" span, to carry tanks.
2 Bridges 30' span to carry all traffic except tanks.
40 R.S. Joists 10" x 5" x 20'0".

The 21' 6" bridge will be erected at No. 3 by the 130th Field Coy. As the abutments still exists, though possibly damaged, no extensions should be necessary.

The 30'0" span Bridges will be erected at Bridges Nos. 1 and 4, by the 106th and 105th Field Companies respectively. These Bridges will probably require extensions, as the abutments are most likely blown. As the bridge will not carry tanks, 6 R.S. Joists will be sufficient for each extension, placed to take the wheels of road tractors. That is to say, each of these two bridges may require 12 joists.

Bridges Nos. 1, 3 and 4 are to be completed first. When the 130th. Field Company have completed No. 3, it will take No. 2 in hand. The Bridge must be constructed to carry tanks, with any material in the Bridging Park not required for Nos. 1, 3 and 4; and with material found locally.

7.   On the morning of 17/10/1918, the C.R.E. 25th Division will have a report Centre at P.17.a.8.3.

Arrangements must be made that reconnoitring parties of Field Coys. can arrive at Bridge Sites, 1 hour after Zero; and advance working parties from Field Companies also, if circumstances permit work at that hour. The remainder of the Field Coys. Sections with tool-carts and pontoon wagons will start so that they can arrive at Bridging sites 2 hours after Zero. The first loads of Bridging materials will not be wanted until Zero plus 2½ hours.

The C.R.E. will endeavour to inform Field Coys at the report centre at P.17.a.8.3. as to the progress of the attack. O.C. Coys. will keep themselves informed however by observation and by keeping touch with forward Brigade Report Centres as to the earliest moment when work can be put in hand; and will act on their own initiative in this matter.

The Company 11th South Lancs. (Pioneers) will remain in their bivouacs (less 1 N.C.O. and 20 men required at Zero hour at the Bridging Park) until they receive notice from the Field Coys. concerned that they are required. As No. 3 Bridge has not been blown, it is not anticipated that the 130th. Field Company will require labour at this point. The Bridges Nos. 1 and 4 will require labour; and O.C. Company Pioneers will have half his Company ready to proceed to each of these places when called on by the O.C's. 106th and 105th Field Coys. respectively.

8.   For transport of material from Bridging Park to site, 6 lorries with 12 trailers will be available - i.e. two lorries with trailers for each Field Company to start with. Trailers to be loaded over night with the material required first, under supervision of C.C. Companies concerned. These lorries are to be returned to 4th. Army Bridging School, as soon as they are no longer required.

9.   ACKNOWLEDGE.

R.J. DONE, Lieut.Col., R.E.
C.R.E., 25th Division

LIST OF MATERIALS FROM
4TH ARMY BRIDGING SCHOOL

No.   2 - 30'0" Span, Class A, steel girder bridge complete with decking sills, etc.

No.   1 - 21'6" Span, Class A, reinforced (to carry tanks), complete with decking sills, etc.

No.   24 - 3'0" steel cubes, complete with sleepers, bolts, etc., to form 6 Crib Piers.

No.   20 - 10" x 5" x 20'0" long R.S. Joists or more if transport is available.

No.   6 - Rollers for launching.
[25th Division C.R.E. War Diary]

Place	Date	Hour	Summary of Events and Information
	16/10		Orders were received to move the Battalion to forward area; the assembly of Battalion was as und 2 Coys in Railway Cutting South of MOUROIS and 1 Coy at P.17.a.central. East of REUMONT preparatory to work in connection with operations by XIII, Corps on Le CATEAU Sector on 17/10/18.
	17/10		1 N.C.O. & 40 men worked on the Bridging Park under C.E. Corps for purpose of loading Lorries Remainder of Company standing to waiting orders. Later the party on the Bridging Park was increased to half Company.
			1 Company worked in reliefs on Railway Bridge, clearing road at Q.15.b.4.1. Work on this job was carried on overnight in half Company reliefs.
			2 Coys under orders of C.E. Corps carried out work on clearing of the MARETZ - LE CATEAU Road.
			Half Coy working on Bridge No 1 Le Cateau with R.E.s.
	18/10		Headquarters Details moved to Billets at HONNECHY.
			1 Coy worked on clearing of debris at Railway Bridge, also cleared Road Le Cateau from K.34.a.6.2. to Bridge. No 1 after which they joined B.H.Q. in Billets at HONNECHY.
			1 Coy still located at Bridging Park. Half Coy of which worked on Bridge No.1 at Le CATEAU.
	19/10		Battalion moved from HONNECHY to ST. BENIN.
			The party working at the Bridging Park and on Bridge No 1 were relieved in the afternoon by the Sussex Pioneer Bn. After relief the party joined us at ST BENIN.
			1 Company proceeded to work on following roads in 8 hour reliefs commencing at 19.00

Place	Date	Hour	Summary of Events and Information

hours.

(i) Q.22.a.6.4. - Q.4.b.5.0.
(ii) Q.4.b.5.0. - Q.17.d.
(iii) Q.4.b.5.0. - K.34.d. thence South to Q.18.d.B.4.
(iv) Q.18.d.8.4 - BAZUEL.

The adjoining roads were also reconnoitered and reports forwarded to the C.R.E. 25th Division. The above Company was relieved and work continued on the same roads up to 13.00 hours 20/10/18.

20/10 — Relief again took place by a further Company at 13.00 hours, but the majority of the labour was concentrated on Q.14.b.5.0. Southwards to Q.17.d.

Orders received to work on fallen bridge at Q.4.d.5.0. This work was very important and half Company reliefs were carried out night and day commencing at 17.00 hours in 4 hour shifts.

21/10 — On the 21st work was still being carried on by reliefs.

1 Company assisting the 182 Tunnelling Coy R.E. on the Flank Road Deviation in Q.5.c.

22/10 — Work still continued on the above Bridge and Plank deviation.

The 11th South Lancs. (Pioneers) commenced on 20/10/18 to clear the block at Q.5.d.5.0. This Battalion put in some excellent work clearing this block. They worked continuously in 6 hours reliefs and finally got the block clear for lorry traffic on the morning of 22nd October. One Company of this Battalion helped to complete the corduroy road which was also finished about this time.
[25th Division C.R.E. War Diary]

Place	Date	Hour	Summary of Events and Information
	23/10		In connection with operations to be carried out by the 3rd & 4th Armies, the following work was allotted to the Battalion.

1 Coy to clear Block at Railway Bridge at R.1.d.0.4. so that road from K.35.d.6.0. to R.8.b.6.5. BAZUEL was practicable for all Transport.

1 Coy on road from K.35.d.6.0. to POMMEREUIL Road to be opened for all traffic, including 6" Guns Mk VII.

1 Coy to open road from BAZUEL through R.3.a.central to POMMEREUIL and also ensure the road from Q.18.a.9.4. through BAZUEL kept open for all traffic.

All forward roads were reconnoitered closely behind the Advance and work carried out immediately on the roads as far as the advance would permit.

Roads detailed and worked upon as far as possible.

(i) K.35.d.6.0. - BAZUEL at R.8.a.9.5.
(ii) L.20.b.2.0. - G.2.c.4.0.
(iii) L.16.b.5.3. - G.13.b.9.5.
(iv) L.26.d.9.4. - L.20.b.2.0.
(v) L.26d.9.4. - L.29.a.4.4.

The whole of the roads detailed above were working upon as far as Advance permitted, and kept open for all traffic during the day. Reports were prepared by Reconnoitering parties and forwarded the C.R.E. 25th Division.

| | 24/10 | | 1 Company worked on Forward roads. |

1 Company worked on Fallen girder bridge at R.1.d.0.4. in half Coy reliefs.

1 Coy remained in Camp in Reserve. This Company relieved the Company working on the Fallen Girder Bridge in the evening.

Place	Date	Hour	Summary of Events and Information
	25/10 to 26/10		Work on the above carried out. Headquarters moved from ST BENIN to LE CATEAU, 2 Coys joining us there after work that day on Defensive Support Positions. 1 Company located at R.1.d.0.2.
	26/10		2 Coys worked on Defensive Support Line which was prepared and taped out by the C.R.E.
			G.1.d. central - G.1.d.8.4. G.2.c.0.3. - G.2.c.1.0. - G.8.a.2.7. thence along contour crossing the road from FONTAINE to G.15.b. a few yards S.E. of the Red Tree, thence to about G.7.c.3.5.
	27/10		1 Company employed on clearing of Block at R.1.d.0.4.
			2 Coys employed on Defensive Support Positions.
	28/10		The Defensive Support Position was amended and taped out by the Commanding Officer. New line taped out was from Road at G.8.a.3.7. via G.8.a.5.4. & G.8.a.4.0. across road to G.8.c.3.9.
			2 Coys employed on the above Defensive Support Position. 1 Coy on clearing of Block at R.1.d.0.4.
	29/10		Works as above carried out.
	30/10		1 Coy clearing road at R.1.d.0.4. forward. 1 Coy repairing road L.16.central - L.29.a. and L.24.a.0.0. cleaning of roads from Q.4.d.6.0. to Q.4.b.5.0. and the road from K.35.d.6.0. to L.29.a.
			1 Company completing work in hand on the Defensive Support Positions.
			After work, one Company changed billets and moved to HONNECHY preparatory to being employed in Operations to be undertaken at a later date.
			[d. Pte. 21368 William Grounds]
	31/10		1 Coy working on Bridging at R.1.d.0.4. which opened for all traffic.
			1 Coy working on Forward Roads. 1 Coy located

Place	**Date**	**Hour**	**Summary of Events and Information**

at HONNECHY (Training).

Dispositions of the Battalion on 31/10/18.

Bn. Hd. Qrs. Transport and 1 Company at ST. BENIN. 1 Company at R.1.d.0.4. 1 Company at HONNECHY. Sheet 57 B used for all Map references.

Casualties incurred.

2nd Lieut. R. CARR & 32574 L.C. LORD S Missing 23/10/18 whilst reconnoitering forward roads last seen 6 pm 23/10/18.

Lieut. H.V. Worrall wounded 26/10/18.

9 O.R.s wounded and 1 O.R. Wounded (Gas) during the period under review.

C C Champion   Lieut. Colonel.
cdg. 11th Bn. South Lancashire Regt (Pioneers)

On the 30th October information was received that at an early date, as part of major operations by the 4th Army, the 25th Division would be expected to cross the SAMBRE-OISE CANAL, capture LANDRECIES and drive the enemy towards the LEVAL Railway.
Work on the Support Line was stopped; and in view of the strenuous time in front of them all Field Companies R.E. and Pioneers were withdrawn into rest billets.
105th. Field Company R.E. went to HONNECHY. 106th. Field Company R.E. to ST. BENIN. 130th. Field Company R.E. to LE CATEAU. The 11th South Lancs (Pioneers) went to St. BENIN with One Company at HONNECHY and One Company at R.1.d.0.4.
[25th Division C.R.E. War Diary]

SECRET   C.R.E. 25th Div.No. 13/50

O.C. 105th. Field Company R.E.
O.C. 106th. Field Company R.E.
O.C. 130th. Field Company R.E.
O.C. 11th. South Lancs (Pioneers).
O.C. No. 2 Sect. (182nd. Tun. Coy. R.E.).

     The following are the arrangements in detail for the R.E. and Pioneers programme in the forthcoming operations.

I.   SECTION, 182nd. TUNNELLING COY. R.E.

     A party consisting of 1 N.C.O. and 10 Men, for saving and demining the bridge and Lock at LANDRECIES.

     3 Men for the wooden bridge about G.17.d.7.7. and 3 men for the foot bridges about G.22.d.0.5.

     These three parties will report to 75th. Brigade Hd.Qrs. at 10.00 hours on 'Y' day.

     The LANDRECIES Bridge party and the G.22.d.0.5. party will advance with the 1/5th. GLOSTERS.

     The G.17.d.7.7. party will advance with the 1/8th. WARWICKS.

     The remainder of the Tunnelling Coy's. Section will search roads, etc. for mines as already detailed.

     The Section less Special Parties may remain in LE CATEAU for Y, Z, night, starting on 'Z' morning in time to reach our present line about G.14.b. at Zero plus 2 hours.

INTENTION. To save the bridges over the SAMBRE-OISE Canal, if possible, and to ensure unmined forward routes for Tanks and Transport.

II.   11th. SOUTH LANCS. (PIONEERS).

     'B' Company 11th. South Lancs. working with 105th Field Company R.E. to ferry over the SAMBRE-OISE Canal. For details of assembly and rendezvous see subsequent para.

     'C' Company work on forward roads as already detailed, this Company will move on 'Y' day to Railway Cutting at R.1.e. and will march on 'Z' morning in time to start work from our present front line at G.14.b. at Zero plus 2 hours.

The remaining Company 11th. South Lancs. (Pioneers) and Advanced Battn. Hd.Qrs., will move on 'Z' morning to neighbourhood of L.27.a.Central, to arrive there at Zero plus 1 hour.

III.   The C.E. XIII Corps Advanced Bridging Dump is at L.27.c.0.8.

IV.   105th. FIELD COMPANY R.E. PLUS 'B' COMPANY (PIONEERS).

The 105th. Field Company R.E. will complete the manufacture by the evening of 1st. November of 84 Petrol Tin rafts and 95 bays of decking at HONNECHY STATION Dump. Of these 4 piers and 5 bays will be used for demonstration on 2nd November.

The 72 bays of decking will be transported from HONNECHY to the 2nd. Supply Tank Company, with sufficient lashings to secure them on 4 Supply Tanks, at BAZEUL, by lorry , to arrive at the Tank rendezvous BAZEUL, at 15.00 hours on 2nd November. The remaining rafts and superstructure will be transported from HONNECHY STATION to three forward dumps under arrangements of O.C., 105th. Field Company R.E., on evening of 2nd. November. For this purpose the 130th and 106th Field Coys. R.E. will send all available pontoon wagons unloaded with teams complete, to report to O.C., 105th. Field Company R.E. at Noon 2nd November. After transporting this Bridging equipment, pontoon wagons will return to their own Units and be reloaded with their equipment and all pontoon wagons and bridging equipment complete with teams and personnel are then at the disposal of O.C., 106th Field Coy. R.E.

O.C., 105th Field Coy. R.E. will arrange to transport the 4 piers and 5 bays required for the demonstration.

On the morning of 'Y' day the 105th Field Coy. R.E. and 'B' Coy. 11th South Lancs (Pioneers) will move to neighbourhood of L.26.a. and on the evening of 'Y' day will move to position of assembly according to detailed arrangement already made with 75th. Inf. Bde.

The detail arrangement for the distribution of rafts, etc., and subsequent advance have been made with 75th. Inf. Bde. The 4 Supply Tanks carrying superstructure plus 6 - 9" x 5" planks to each tank, will move in their own time in such a way that the tanks will arrive South of the Road at G.16.d.0.4. at Zero plus 4 hours. O.C., 130th Field Coy. R.E. will send 3 sappers with each Tank as an off-loading party. These Sappers will report to the Supply Tank Company at BAZEUL at 15.00 hours on 2nd November.

In case of breakdown of a Tank O.C., 130th Field Coy. R.E. will be prepared and will be responsible to carry the superstructure forward with his own horse transport.

V.   130th. FIELD COMPANY R.E.

After the 4 Supply Tanks have been off-loaded of their Bridging superstructure they will rendezvous empty about G.16.c.Central.

The 130th. Field Coy. R.E. will construct 2 light trussed foot bridges 22 feet long and will arrange to transport them with his own transport on evening of 2nd November to a forward dump. He will also provide a party of Sappers to carry these Bridges with the 1st. wave of the 1/5th Glosters.

INTENTION.   In case the lock at LANDRECIES is standing or is partially demolished these 2 foot bridges will be placed by the sappers to enable the Infantry to cross at this point.

The carrying party will report to 75th Inf. Bde. H.Q. at 10.00 hours on 'Y' day. Further details of assembly and advance of these 2 foot bridges will be made direct by O.C., 130th Field Coy. with the 75th Inf Bde. and O.C., 1/5th GLOSTERS.

Apart from Special Parties already detailed the 130th Field Coy. R.E. is allotted the task of bridging the PETITE HELPE RIVER. For this purpose the 4 Supply Tanks are available provided they can cross the SAMBRE-OISE Canal. There is also available the Bridging Equipment of the 66th Division and the cork light Infantry bridging material.

The Bridging Equipment of the 66th Division will report to O.C. 130th Field Coy. R.E. at neighbourhood of Bridging Dump L.27.o.0.8. at 06.00 hours on 'Z' day.

The 130th Field Company R.E. will move to the neighbourhood of L.27.o.0.8. to arrive there at Zero plus 4 hours.

O.C., 130th Field Company R.E. may have to transport with horse transport the cork bridging material from the Bridging Dump L.27.o.0.8. to the Tank rendezvous about G.16.c.Cent. and to load the Tanks with it.

For this purpose the bridging wagons and teams of the 66th Divn. will be available.

INTENTION.   If the LANDRECIES Bridge is crossable by Tanks, to load the Tanks with the cork bridging material and get the loaded Tanks to the S.E. side of the Canal as soon as possible.

If the bridge is damaged, but it appears practicable to repair it sufficiently to take Tanks during the night of 'Z' day, to load the tanks with the cork bridging material and get them across in time for further advance.

In either of the above cases the Supply Tanks would accompany the advance to the PETITE HELPE RIVER, the 130th Field Coy. R.E. finding parties to go with them to construct Light Infantry Bridges over the PETITE HELPE RIVER; this operation being followed by the 66th. Division pontoon equipment for pontooning the river.

If however the LANDRECIES Bridge be so destroyed that Tanks will be unable to cross it during the night after 'Z' day it will be necessary to send the Light Bridging Material by pontoon wagon to the PETITE HELPE RIVER. As there will be plenty of time to ascertain the state of affairs before the further advance takes place definite instructions will be given to O.C., 130th Field Coy. R.E. during 'Z' day.

VI.   106th. FIELD COMPANY R.E.

106th. Field Coy. R.E. will construct two pontoon bridges, up stream and down stream of the LANDRECIES Bridge to be available for Field Guns and Horse Transport at Zero plus 7 hours.

106th. Field Coy. R.E. will move on 'Y' day to neighbourhood of POMMEREUIL.

O.C., 106th. Field Coy. R.E. has at his disposal all the Bridging Equipment of the 25th. Division.

Bridging wagons are not to move forward during daylight.

Two G.S. wagons carrying 4 Artillery Bridges for making approach bridges are placed at the disposal of O.C., 106th. Field Coy. R.E.

R.J. DONE, Lieut.Col., R.E.
C.R.E., 25th Division

1st. NOVEMBER, 1918.

Issued at 15.30 hours.

[25th Division C.R.E. War Diary]

Place	Date	Hour	Summary of Events and Information
	01/11		The Battalion was rested this day pending forthcoming operations, and all men were occupied in Special Training with the exception of 'A' Coy who were located near BAZUEL and responsible the keeping open of the road from POMMEREUIL to FONTAINE for all traffic.
	02/11		Dispositions as on the 31/10/18. Special training for all Battalion except one Coy responsible for the maintenance of main POMMEREUIL - FONTAINE Road for all traffic and a special party detailed for the 105th Field Coy R.E. to unload lorries from dump for the Bridging Park.
			There was a practice and demonstration Nr ST BENIN for the crossing of the SAMBRE-OISE CANAL a portion of the work being allotted to 'B' Coy who were working in conjunction with 105th Field Coy R.E., 25th Division.
			[d.o.w. Pte. 204919 Henry Hagger]
	03/11		November 3rd 1918 was known as "Y" Day and in accordance with Operation Orders received movements as under were completed. 'B' Coy together with 105th Field Coy R.E. moved from HONNECHY to their forward positions at L.26.a. and at dusk moved to assembly positions in Front Line, after which all materials were drawn from the advance dumps already prepared by 'A' Coy. 'B' Coy with the R.Es were ready at midnight with the Infantry to commence the advance at ZERO hour which was at 5.45 am on the 4th.
			'C' Coy moved from ST. BENIN to the Railway Cutting in front of LE CATEAU.
			Advance B.H.Q. opened at POMMEREUIL at 18.00 hours and on Z. day advanced Report Centre moved at 05.00 hours at MALGARNI with 75th B.H.Q.
	04/11		A call was made on the Coy in reserve to supply 1

Place	Date	Hour	Summary of Events and Information
			Platoon to maintain and keep open the Road POMMEREUIL to FONTAINE, particularly at FORRESTERS HOUSE & MALGARNI which was being heavily shelled. The Officer and 2 O.Rs reconnoitering the work were all wounded. Work commenced at 8.30 am. on Z day also 1 Platoon warned to be held in readiness for work with the 130th Field Coy R.E. for the purpose of assisting in bridging of the PETIE HELPE RIVER.
			Report received that O.C. 'C' Coy (Capt M.D. Robinson) was wounded and heavy shelling experienced during assembly. Work on Forward roads progressed well and Road party supplied men to assist R.E. Coy on approaches for two Pontoon bridges across Canal at LANDRECIES LOCK.
			Orders received to move the whole of the Battalion (less 'B' Coy) to FONTAINE au BOIS. Rear H.Q. Q.M. Stores, Transport & Coy Details accordingly moved forward at 8 pm from ST. BENIN. 'A' Coy remained for the night in Bivouacs near POMMEREUIL. 1 Platoon of 'A' Coy ordered at 10.15 pm to proceed to report to O.C. 130th Field Coy R.E. at L.18.a.8.6. for work until further orders.
			Capt. M.D.ROBINSON 4th S.Lancs. Attd. Wounded. 2/Lt. H.JONES 5th Bn. Attd. Wounded. 2/Lt. J.KIRKPATRICK 5th Bn. Attd. Wounded. Lt. L.HENSHAW Wounded at duty. [25th Division A&Q War Diary]
			[d.o.w. C.S.M. 16443 James Leigh; k.i.a. Pte. 49314 Reginald Andrews, Pte. 241151 Edward Greenough, Pte. 48996 Frank Rogers, L/Cpl. 204914 Percy Russell, Pte. 46601 Hezekiah Rylance, L/Cpl. 34080 Percival Townsend]
	05/11		The 25th Division attacked on the 4/11/18 and Zero hour for the attack was at 5.45 am. The 25th Division were required to cross SAMBRE A

Place	**Date**	**Hour**	**Summary of Events and Information**

L'OISE and capture LANDRECIES and to capture further objectives which involve the crossing of PETITE HELPE RIVER. The following is the detail of work for this Battalion in connection with the above operations.

'B' Coy with the 105th Field Coy R.E. to ferry over the SAMBRE-OISE Canal. This operation was successfully completed and the Company then moved back to neighbourhood of POMMEREUIL.

'A' Coy at Zero plus 1 hour moved to L.28.a. and were held in reserve. This Coy supplied 3 N.C.O.s & 24 men to work with 'B' Coy bridging the SAMBRE-OISE CANAL.

'C' Coy were detailed to work on forward roads as under.

Coy moved on 'Y' day from ST. BENIN to Railway Cutting in vicinity of R.1.c.

They marched on 'Z' morning in time to start work from our present front line on that date at G.14 at Zero plus 2 hours.

Roads worked on - The POMMEREUIL - L.29.a. - MALGARAI - L.19.a.7.8. - G.13.d.7.0. - G.14.c.4.4. - G.20.a.9.5. - G.15.d.6.4. route.

MALGARAI-le-FAUX - G.13.b.9.8. - G.20.a.8.6.

Le FAUX - FONTAINE-AUS-BOIS - FAUBOURG - BOYERES - LANDRECIES and subsequent to the crossing of the canal, forward roads as follows:- MALGARAI-le-Faux - LANDRECIES Rd, with special attention to road Junction and railway crossing in G.16.d.

Along the roads - Min Road LANDRECIES to MAROILLES and the road LANDRECIES - LA BLANCHISSERIE to OLD MILL DEPRES.

'B' Coy moved forward to FONTAINE au BOIS. Work carried as under on this date.

Place	Date	Hour	Summary of Events and Information
			1 Coy filling in crater & making corduroy track West of LANDRECIES on LANDRECIES-MAROILLES Main Road.
			2 Coys clearing, draining & repairing main LANDRECIES-MAROILLES Rd.
			[d.o.w. Pte. 16525 John Boardman]
	06/11		1 Coy employed making approaches to Pontoon Bridges Les Mill Despres. This Company moved MAROILIE after work. 1 Platoon with 130 Field Coy R.E. bridging.
			1 Coy moved to LANDRECIES and worked there on craters & roads. In the afternoon Coy moved to MAROILLES.
			1 Coy worked on roads in front of LANDRECIES and billetted in the town.
			B.H.Q. moved in the morning from FONTAINE au BOIS to LANDRECIES and in the afternoon received orders to move immediately to MAROILLES with 2 Coys. This was done.
			[d.o.w. Pte. 42248 Leonard Parkey, Pte. 49067 Thomas Smith]
	07/11		1 Platoon Bridging with 130th Field Coy R.E. 3 Platoons on Bridge at DOMPIERRE J.2.a.0.3.
			1 Coy working on MARBAIX ROAD. Coy moved to TASMIERES.
			1 Coy moved from LANDRECIES to MAROILLE in the morning and moved on to DOMPIERRE the afternoon.
	08/11		Coy worked on Craters on LANDRECIES-MAROILLES Rd. This Coy moved back to MAROILLES in order to be nearer the work and the 1 Platoon which had up to then been with the 130th Field Coy R.E. joined them there.
			1 worked on Bridge and new road at ROSIERES.
			1 Coy worked on Corduroy track and crater in

Place	Date	Hour	Summary of Events and Information

DOMPIERRE railway Station.

09/11   Work carried out as on the 8/11/18.

Casualties incurred during the Operations under review as under:-

Officers wounded.
Lieut. H.V. Worrall. 26/10/18.
2nd Lieut. N. Carr. Missing 22/10/18.
Captain M.O. Robinson. Wounded 4/11/18.
2nd Lt. H. Jones. Wounded 4/11/18 (Died of wounds). 2nd Lt. Kirkpatrick. Wounded 4/11/18.
Lieut. L. Henshaw. Wounded still duty 4/11/18.

O.Rs. Killed 6. O.Rs Wounded 32. Wounded still duty 2.

C C Champion   Lieut. Colonel.
 cdg. 11th Bn. South Lancashire Regt (Pioneers)

NARRATIVE OF OPERATIONS 0F 105th FIELD CO. R.E.
BETWEEN 1st and 10th NOVEMBER 1918.

BATTLE OF LANDRECIES

Nov. 1st-2nd. Manufacture continued and completed by about midday 2nd November. Each float was provided with 2 breast lines of 12 fathoms and a light paddle, the whole firmly secured for carrying.

On night of 2nd November floats and part of duckboards were transported to assembly dumps by Pontoon Wagons (Wagons of two other Companies assisted in this). This was an important part of the operation, as everything depended on assembling the stores at these dumps (as near as possible to actual assembly positions of attacking troops) with as many as possible intact. The usual heavy shelling of this area at night was encountered but only one wagon was hit - the whole team of 3 drivers and 6 horses being hit, but only 5 of the 10 floats.

On the afternoon of the 2nd November a demonstration was given at ST. BENIN - a platoon of Worcesters attacked across the SELLE - Sapper N.C.O's being used as carrying party for floats etc. Six floats were used. The general impression was that the floats were good and that the rafting in particular was successful. (These 6 floats were sent up on night 3/4th to replace those damaged).

The crossing divided itself naturally into 3 separate parties.

(1) Crossing of SAMBRE RIVER in right Battalion Sector (this to be done by forming foot bridges direct).

(2) Crossing of SAMBRE CANAL S.W. of LANDRECIES (in case of first Battalion - rafting).

(3) Crossing of SAMBRE CANAL N.E. of LANDRECIES (in case of first Battalion - rafting).

The whole was therefore organised in 3 bridging parties numbered 1 - 3 for 1 - 3 tasks respectively, and following allotment of stores made:-

No. 1 party. 18 floats
18 duckboards for forming 3 foot bridges across

SAMBRE RIVER.
10 floats for commencement of crossing of
Canal.

No. 2 party. 20 floats for crossing of CANAL - making a
total of 30 floats on the CANAL S.W. of
LANDRECIES.

No. 3 party. 35 floats for crossing N.E. of LANDRECIES.
(72 duckboards were conveyed to RIVER at
zero plus 3 hours by Supply Tanks for forming
foot bridges for crossing of remainder of 75th
Brigade.

The whole were subdivided into Bridging Sections each of 5
floats, under a Sapper N.C.O. assisted by Pioneer N.C.O. Each
float had 2 Pioneers for carrying and 1 Sapper, who was primarily
intended for paddling the float across the CANAL (he was also
responsible for clearing of gaps during the advance). No. 1 party
had 18 additional Pioneers for carrying the duckboards.

Each of the three bridging parties was under the command of a
R.E. Subaltern assisted by 2 Pioneer Officers. The total
personnel of each party was therefore as follows:-

	Officers		N.C.O's		Spr. Orderlies	Sprs.	Pions.	Total
	R.E.	Pions.	R.E.	Pions.				
1.	1	2	5	5	2	25	50+18	108
2.	1	2	4	4	2	20	40	73
3.	1	2	7	7	2	35	70	124
H.Q.	1	1	-	-	4	-	-	6
	4		16		10	80		311

TOTAL R.E. PERSONNEL 110

No. 1 Party was under the command of 2nd Lieut.
A.L.ARMSTRONG

No. 2 Party was under the command of 2nd Lieut. WELLS R.E.

No. 3 Party was under the command of 2nd Lieut. J.M.PETTY
R.E.

(This Officer also had with him about 14 Sappers of 130th Field Co. R.E. who made up deficiencies in No. 2 Party.)

Nov. 3rd.   A map is attached shewing assembly positions and boundaries etc. of operations. (not attached).

On morning of the 3rd the Field Co. with "B" Co. 11th SOUTH LANCS. (PIONEERS) marched from HONNECHY at 08.00 hours arriving at near assembly positions N. of POMMEREUIL at 11.00 hours. At 11.30 hours combined parade was held and the whole organised with their numbered bridging sections (there had been no previous opportunity for this; the halt was primarily intended to enable the men to get a hot meal).

At 13.30 hours Companies paraded in Bridging Sections and moved off to forward area.

Pioneer Officers and Sapper N.C.O's had previously reconnoitred forward assembly positions with Battalions concerned.

No. 1 Party to assemble with rear Co. of right Battn.
1/5th Gloucesters.

No. 2 Party to assemble with rear Co. of left Battn.
1/8th Warwicks.

No. 3 Party to assemble with right front Co. of support Battn.
1/8th Worcesters.

By 16.30 hours troops were in the vicinity of assembly positions - the rear parties encountering a considerable amount of shelling. (By good fortune the shelling accompanying enemy counter attack on right flank Division during the morning had died down).

From this time on H.Q. of Field Company was at H.Q. of 1/5th Gloucesters, and Officers Commanding Bridging Parties were responsible for the assembling of their parties.

The Officers had instructions that when troops had reached their assembly position, a suitable opportunity would be chosen after dusk for drawing bridging material from their respective dumps.

No. 1 Party had completed this by 20.00 hours and had dug in. There was a slight alteration of assembly position for this party at about midnight, and they moved forward and to the left in order to conform with the Coy. of 1/5th Gloucesters.

No. 2 Party had instructions to wait for the assembly of the first Coy. of 1/8th Worcesters. The actual details of this were not clear until about 02.00 hours on the 4th. This Coy. together with No. 2 bridging party were to assemble behind road running parallel to and 200 yards in rear of front assembly line, and at zero turn right into file and march up the road. This appeared to me to be unwise from several points of view, and on representation being made to the Commanding Officer 1/8th Worcesters this was altered and assembly was ordered to be made in front of road and the advance would be in line across country. No. 2 party were then ordered to assemble in the first position occupied by No. 1 party. This was reported complete at 04.15 hours on the 4th.

No. 3 party reported at 2000 hours on the 3rd that all bridging material was assembled in jumping off position, and the troops were resting near at hand in cellars in LE FAUX. They moved out to jumping off position at 04.30 hours on the 4th.

Nov. 4th. Zero was at 06.15 hours.

The attack was through very close country. A heavy mist came down before zero and added to the difficulty of maintaining direction.

The enemy barrage after zero was not heavy and nearly all the troops and bridging parties got through it with little trouble; but part of Corps on right and French had attacked at 05.45 hours, and during the 30 minutes following enemy shelled our assembly positions heavily. Bridging parties fortunately suffered few casualties.

Precautions had been taken to assemble the whole of the attacking troops as close as possible up to the front tape, with the intention of opening up to greater distances in depth, when through enemy barrage. The difficult conditions at the time prevented this being done, and the bridging parties (1 and 2 particularly) became involved in the fighting. Fortunately, however, the parties suffered few casualties in this way, and were of considerable assistance to the Infantry in lending weight to the attack and in clearing gaps - the Sappers of these parties took considerable numbers of prisoners.

No. 3 party appeared to have gone straight through to the CANAL without heavy opposition, arriving at the CANAL at about 10.10 hours. 2nd Lieut. PETTY with a Platoon of 1/8th

Warwicks without an Officer were the first troops down to the railway embankment. The Infantry remained there and the bridging parties proceeded to the CANAL. The first Infantry (Warwicks) arrived at the CANAL at about 10.30 hours. The first Co. was then rafted across. Two foot bridges were completed by 11.30 hours. Most of this work including carrying of duckboards from Tanks was done under considerable M.G. fire and shelling. On completion of this work parties were withdrawn, leaving maintenance party. Casualties were not heavy. (30 floats of the party arrived at the CANAL, remainder being temporarily lost).

No. 1 party with 1/5thGloucesters were held up just in front of light railway by heavy shelling, M.G. and T.M. fire. Two Tanks arrived and cleared this situation and the attack then went forward to the CANAL with little opposition. The bridge across the SAMBRE RIVER had been charged but not blown, and was only partially damaged by shell fire. Sergt WOOD with a Sapper were the first to arrive there and withdrew the charge. When the Infantry began to cross, however, the enemy brought a M.G. into action and necessitated the forming of a foot bridge farther upstream. 15 Floats had been allotted for making 3 bridges across the stream, but only 9 were required. (2 bridges in addition to the one left standing were considered sufficient). The remaining 12 (21 reached the CANAL with this party, remaining 4 arrived later) were taken up to the CANAL. Here the enemy had left one foot bridge intact. First Infantry crossed on this. 2nd Lieut. ARMSTRONG immediately sent a carrying party to the rendezvous of the Supply Tanks for the duckboards, and he was told that under the circumstances two float bridges would be sufficient.

No. 2 party arrived at the CANAL shortly after No. 1 with 17 floats intact.

By 12.00 hours these two bridges were complete, and No. 2 party had also repaired a second German bridge making a total of 4 foot bridges on this side.

These parties withdrew immediately this work was complete, leaving maintenance parties.

Company spent night 4/5th at POMMEREUIL.

Casualties during the operations were:-

	Officers	O.R.
R.E	-	7 wounded.
Pioneers	1 (wounded) (at duty)	4 killed 2 died of wounds. 13 wounded.

Nov. 5th.   Orders received to move to vicinity of LANDRECIES and move was carried out during the afternoon.

At about 23.00 hours orders received to join 7th Infantry Brigade at MAROILLES to continue advance on 6th.

Nov. 6th.   No. 1 Section was sent to report to O.C. Advance Guard 20th Manchesters at 06.30 hours.

Remainder of Co. marched with main body of Brigade. At about 11.30 hours report received from O.C. No. 1 Section asking for Pontoon and Trestles to bridge Gd. HELPE on TAISNIERES - DOMPIERRE road. Earlier report had been received that road bridge had been blown and trestles and pontoons were ready to go forward. The Gd. HELPE was bridged by pontoons in time for the crossing of transport of advance guard. At the same time a G.S. trestle bridge was commenced and completed at about 15.00 hours. This was fortunate as the river began to rise rapidly, and by 16.00 hours the on shore bays of pontoon bridge rendered it useless.

Infantry reached E. edge of DOMPIERRE along line of railway before night.

Company returned to billets at BASSE NOYELLES for the night.

During the night orders were received to send Officer to reconnoitre:-

     (1) Gap at bridge at DOMPIERRE STATION.

     (2) River bridge at HUGEMONT.

Sergt. Wood and Capt. RIDGE were sent out for this.

Nov. 7th.   Advance was continued. Company remaining at disposal of 7th Infantry Brigade. No. 4 Section was sent with the advance guard

- 21st Manchesters.

As soon as advance commenced No. 4 Section put in had a diversion at DOMPIERRE STATION for horsed transport.

Road bridge 1000 yards S.E. of Station was found to be heavily charged and ready for blowing. Charges were removed.

Remainder of Company had at first been employed in dismantling <u>Pontoon Bridge</u> at TAISNIERES, and improving diversion to Trestle Bridge. They were brought forward to DOMPIERRE STATION at about 12.00 hours. Pioneer Company arrived to assist during the afternoon - they were employed partly on road diversion and partly on filling crater at star road 1100 yards N.E. of Station.

On the night 7/8th 25th Division was relieved by 66th Division.

The C.R.E. had visited the work during the day and ordered a lorry route diversion through DOMPIERRE STATION to be put in hand forthwith. A Field Co. and Pioneer Co. of the 66th Division were also detailed for this and commenced work on the evening of the 7th - owing to the intense darkness night work was impossible.

Night 7/8th Company billeted in DOMPIERRE.

Nov. 8th.	Company worked on and completed corduroy diversion for horsed transport 500 yards S.E. of Station. Pioneer Co. assisted in this - they also continued filling of crater at star roads. One Section assisted Co. of 66th Division on lorry route diversion.
Nov. 9th.	Diversion was open as a 1-way road at about 10.00 hours.
Nov. 10th.	Company took over lorry route diversion from 66th Division; this was practically complete by evening.

7.12.1918.

F W Richards
Major R.E.
O.C. 105th Field Co. R.E.

[25th Division 105th Field Co. R.E. War Diary]

Place	Date	Hour	Summary of Events and Information
Maroilles	07/11		Division relieved in the line by 66th Division. [25th Division A&Q War Diary]
	08/11		R.E. and 11th S Lancs (P) remain working with 66th Division. [25th Division A&Q War Diary]
Landrecies	09/11		Orders issued that no troops are to be billeted in cellars owing to infection from influenza. [25th Division A&Q War Diary]
	10/11		Battalion employed on the cleaning, filling in of Craters &c in the vicinity of Landrecies & Maroilles.
Maroiles	11/11		Battalion moved to Billets at SARS-POTERIES.
			At 07.30 hrs on 11/11/18 wire was received that hostilities would cease at 11.30 hrs that day.
	12/11		Bn employed on work filling in of Craters in vicinity of SARS POTERIES.
	15/11		BHQ & B Coy moved to vicinity of AVESNES where 'C' Coy had moved to on the 13/11/18.
	18/11		Battn moved by march route to ORS staging the night 18/19th at TASNIERES arriving ORS 19th Nov 1918.
	19/11		[d. Pte. 32573 Sydney Lord]
			R.E. and 11th S Lancs (P) returned from 66th Division and billeted as follows. 105 Field Coy LE CATEAU. 106 Field Coy POMMEREUIL. 130 Field Coy LE CATEAU. 11th S Lancs (P) ORS. [25th Division A&Q War Diary]
	20/11		Battn employed on Salving & clearing of devastated area in the vicinity of ORS BAZUEL & POMMEREUIL.
	25/11		Continued work on Salving & clearing of areas.
			[d. Pte. 49142 Henry Foster]
	29/11		Moved to QUIEVY by march route on 2911/18 & continued on clearing & cleaning of Billets

Place	Date	Hour	Summary of Events and Information
			occupied by Battn.
	01/12		Battn still at QUIEVY as per previous report.
	04/12		His Majesty the King passed thro' QUIEVY at about 2.30 pm. The Battalion with the 7th Inf Bde formed up on the side of the road & gave His Majesty 3 cheers. H.M. the King walked along the line & conversed with the officers & men.
	16/12		The Battn moved from QUIEVY to VIESLY & occupied Billets at this latter place on same date.
	17/12		Information recd that the u/m were awarded Immediate Awards for Operations during Nov 1918.

Lt S E Boulton M.C.   Bar to M.C.
Lieut L Henshaw   M.C.
61090 Pte Redstone V.   D.C.M.
204866 Pte S Rumble   M.M.

Place	Date	Hour	Summary of Events and Information
	18/12		115 ORs proceeded to Interviewing Centre Cambrai on date stated in margin for transfer to Army Reserve (Mining).
			On dates other than Wednesday & Saturday afternoons Battalion employed on Training & Salvaging of Area in vicinity of Billets.
	31/12		Strength 34 Officers 582 ORs.

C C Champion   L'Col.
Cdg 11th Bn S Lancs Rgt (Pnrs)

1919

Place	Date	Hour	Summary of Events and Information
	01/01		Battalion located at YIESLEY employed on Salving & training until 12.1.19 when a move from YIESLEY was made to SOLESMES on 13.1.19.
	13/01		Battalion employed on Salvage work up to end of month.
			Demobilization of the men of Battn commenced 18/1/19 & 151 men sent for dispersal up to end of month leaving Battn strength on that date 437 ORs & 33 Officers.
	17/02		The Battalion still at SOLESMES employed on Salvage work.
	18/02		The Battalion moved from SOLESMES to ESCADOEUVRES on this date & occupied Billets at the latter place, and employed on Salvage work.
Escaudoeuvres	26/02 to 28/02		Information received that the undermentioned had been awarded the "MILITARY MEDAL" No 48993 Sergeant H. McCoy.
			Demobilization of the Battalion has progressed steadily throughout the month. Number demobilized during Feby:- 7 Officers & 162 Other Ranks.
			Strength of the Battalion at end of month :- 26 Officers & 255 Other Ranks.
			C C Champion Lt. Colonel. Commanding 11th Bn. South Lancs Regt. (Pioneers)
Escaudoeuvres	01/03		The Battalion still at ESCADOEUVRES employed on Salvage Work.
Escaudoeuvres	22/03		Information received that the undermentioned had been awarded the "Medaille Barbayie si Credin 3rd Class (Roumanian Decoration) No 20015 Private James Marsh.

Place	Date	Hour	Summary of Events and Information
	31/03		38 Other Ranks re-enlisted under A.O. IV of 10/12/18, 35 of which have been finally approved and sent to the U.K. on furlough.
			170 Other Ranks available for the Armies of Occupation under A.O. 55 of 1919 and awaiting disposal, which leaves the Battalion at CADRE Strength.
			Strength of the Battalion at end of month : - 17 Officers & 213 Other ranks.
			C C Champion Lt Colonel Comdg 11th Vn. South Lancs regt. (Pioneers)
Escaudoeuvres	01/04		The Battalion still located at ESCAUDOEUVRES and employed on Salvage work.
	30/04		Total Re-enlistment to date is 41 all of which have been finally approved and sent to the U.K. on re- enlistment furlough.
			The Strength of the Battalion at the end of the month is as follows :-
			Cadre 4 Officers and 41 Other Ranks.
			Personnel eligible for Army of Occupation 144 Other Ranks.
			Volunteers for Army of Occupation 7 Officers Detached from Unit 2 Officers.
			Total 13 Officers and 185 Other Ranks.
			C C Champion Lieut. Colonel Comdg 11th Bn. South Lancs Regt. (Pioneers)
Escaudoeuvres	01/05		The Battalion still located near ESCAUDOEUVRES.
Escaudoeuvres	07/05		2 Officers left the Battalion to report for duty with the 67 P.O.W. Coy ETAPLES.
Escaudoeuvres	17/05		2 Officers left the Battalion to report for duty with the 191 P.O.W. Coy ETAPLES.

1919

Place	Date	Hour	Summary of Events and Information
Escaudoeuvres	27/05		1 Officer & 70 OR's left the Battalion to report for duty with the 67 P.O.W. Coy ETAPLES.
Escaudoeuvres	28/05		1 Officer & 59 OR's left the Battalion to report for duty with the 191 P.O.W. Coy ETAPLES.
			The remainder of OR's eligible for Army of Occupation are employed with the H.Q. Cambrai Sub Area.
Escaudoeuvres	29/05		5 O.R's on reduction of Cadre establishment sent for dispersal.
Escaudoeuvres	31/05		The strength of the Battalion at the end of the month is as follows :- 6 Offs & 38 Other Ranks.
			C C Champion Lieut Colonel Comdg. 11th Bn. South Lancs Regt. (Pioneers)
Escaudoeuvres	01/06		The Battalion Cadre located at Escaudoeuvres.
	06/06		Instructions received for the formation of a Battalion Cadre & and Equipment Guard.
	08/06		The Bn cadre entrained for Cambrai for dispatch to the U.K. Embarked on 12th June 1919.
	13/06		The Bn Equipment Guard entrained at Cambrai Ville with Baggage, Equipment and Wagons for despatch to the U.K.
			Embarked on the 19th June 1919.
			All the Cadre personnel of this Unit on the completion of duties were sent for demobilization.
			C C Champion Lieut. Colonel Comdg. 11th Bn. South Lancs Regt. (Pioneers)

Sources

The Lancashire Infantry Museum

11th Battalion South Lancashire Regiment War Diary
11th Battalion South Lancashire Regiment Nominal Roll of Officers
Personal diary of A. T. Champion

The National Archives

25th Division A&Q War Diary [WO 95/2228]
25th Division CRE War Diary [WO 95/2232]
105th Field Co. R.E. War Diary [WO 95/2235]
30th Division A&Q Extracts [WO 154/45-49]
30th Division A&Q War Diary [WO 95/2315]
30th Division CRE War Diary [WO 95/2320]

The Commonwealth War Graves Commission
http://www.cwgc.org/

Printed in Great Britain
by Amazon

52339010R00111